LIVING SPRINGS

OLIVE WYON

Living Springs

New Religious Movements
in Western Europe

SCM BOOK CLUB
NAPERVILLE, ILL.

In Memory of Mère Geneviève
Foundress of Grandchamp

9·86

FIRST PUBLISHED 1963
© OLIVE WYON 1963
PRINTED IN GREAT BRITAIN BY
BILLING AND SONS LTD
GUILDFORD AND LONDON

CONTENTS

ILLUSTRATIONS

Preface

THIS slight sketch of movements which are beginning to take shape in Western Europe is part of contemporary history. These are movements in which new communities of Christian men and women seek to live a 'religious' life, i.e. a communal life under a Rule. There is a background in history to these contemporary movements, as I have tried to indicate in a brief chapter on the meaning of monasticism. But these religious movements are *new*; in fact, they are part of the ecumenical spirit which is renewing Christianity in our time.

During the last fifty years the doctrine of the Church has come to the fore in a new and living way. As always, it contains the three elements of religion : the historical and institutional, the intellectual and theological, and the spiritual, experimental elements. All these are essential. If one element is overlooked, the life of the Church is weakened—but if the third element, the 'spiritual', is ignored the whole life of the Church is imperilled. It is this third element which is bubbling up afresh from hidden springs, yet not (as so often in the past) leading to separatism and the formation of new sects, but rising within the Church at large (both Catholic and Protestant), renewing her from within and becoming a force for Christian unity.

One of the main difficulties in trying to describe this movement is due to the wealth of material. It has only been possible to present a few illustrative examples. But the more we delve into this subject, the more do we realize how little is known—how much must be happening out of sight.

The author is very grateful to the many people from Britain and other countries who have so generously contributed information about their life and work, and to the leaders of the new Protestant communities in particular : to the Prior of Taizé, who gave her much help, and to the Sisters of Darmstadt. Soeur Geneviève of Grandchamp took the greatest interest in this study from the outset. In addition, the author owes a debt of gratitude to the Rev. A. M. Allchin and the Rev. Victor de Waal for their interest and encouragement, and above all, to her friend and collaborator, Dr G. L. Marsh-Micheli, for her constant and generous assistance.

OLIVE WYON

Cambridge, 1962

Prologue

A FEW miles from Assisi, in the valley of Spoleto, there is one of the most beautiful sights in Italy: the Springs of Clitumnus. The Clitumnus is a small, peaceful river, which waters the flat plain at the foot of the hills, and then winds its way southward, till it merges into the Tiber. There is nothing special about it but the Springs. In pagan days this was a sacred spot, for springs were mysterious, and were revered for their religious significance. The cattle who used to feed in the surrounding meadows were valued as precious sacrifices on great religious occasions. Virgil speaks of them in one of his descriptions of the beauties of Italy:

Hence come white herds of mighty sacrificial bulls,
Washed again and again in Clitumnus' sacred river,
To lead, towards the temples of the gods, the Roman triumphs.

And Propertius, another Roman poet, whose home lay in this district, alludes to the Springs in two lovely lines:

Among the woods where the Clitumnus hides its lovely
springs, and white oxen bathe in the cool stream.

It is still a quiet place, though it lies near the road through the valley. All one sees at first is a tranquil expanse of water, overhung by willows and bordered by poplars. Coming nearer we see a chain of pools, lying under trees. But though the water looks so still at a distance, when we get nearer we see that it is always moving. Moment by moment fresh water keeps bubbling up from each pool and flowing away to form the river. Some of the pools are quite small and shallow; others are larger and deeper. All, large and small, are always being renewed. But the strange thing about them is this: even the smallest cannot be stopped. Quietly they go on and on all the time; if anyone were to try to fill them up with earth and stones they would quietly go round another way and create a fresh pool of equally clear living water. Where have they come from?—for they appear to spring straight out of the bare earth? Looking up to the range of rocky barren hills we realize that this water must have come down from the heights through thousands of unseen hidden channels, to converge at this spot, where these tiny rills come out into the light of day.

It is no wonder that the ancients regarded this as a sacred place: for it is a wonderful experience to see fresh clean water continually bubbling up out of the dry ground, under a hot sun. It reminds us of the 'river of the water of life', 'bright as crystal', flowing from the throne of God, and of the tree of life, whose leaves are 'for the healing of the nations' (Rev. 22.1-2). It reminds us, too, that although there are many seasons of dryness and darkness in the history of the Church, although Christian people have sometimes been on the verge of despair, yet when they least expected it, fresh springs arose in the desert, and 'through the scent of water it was able to bud, and it put forth boughs like a plant' (Job 14.9).

It is of such 'living springs' that this book speaks. Some of them may be very small and apparently insignificant; but whether small or great they are born of the Spirit of God, and they cannot be stopped. Within themselves they bear the promise of renewal for the Church and for the world.

No Church historian has yet given us a study of the way in which 'renewal' comes to the Church. Yet we do not need to be great scholars to know that again and again, when the life of the Church was at a very low ebb, some new element 'intervened' and changed the whole situation. From the purely human point of view these periods of renewal are inexplicable.

Who would have dreamt, for instance, that the little group of students at Oxford who gathered round the Wesley brothers and tried to reform their own lives, amidst mockery and ridicule, would become part of the great Revival which swept the country and was the beginning of a new era? Or that the Church in France, which seemed beaten to the very ground during the Revolution, would rise again in power? Or that the Church in Germany in the 1930s would rise to such a daring resistance to the pagan government, and emerge from this trial stronger than before? Calvin has said that 'the story of the Church is the story of many resurrections!' Though at the present moment there is no sign of a general 'resurrection' in the Church in Western Europe, there are signs of new life which show that here and there the Church is being renewed from within by 'living springs'.

In every case, this 'new life' emerges from a praying group: whether it is called a 'community' or a 'company' or a 'team'. In other words, the 'living water' comes from Christ himself, where two or three meet in his name—and where, as in the first community of Jerusalem, they remain steadfastly together in faith and fellowship, in sacramental life and in prayer. For 'renewal' always comes when we return to the source, to Jesus Christ himself. But all through the course of the history of the Christian Church, this return to the source means going into 'the desert'. It is there, in solitude and silence, that the voice of God is heard; it is there that the river of prayer is born, that prayer which is the life-blood of the Church.

So we begin the story of new movements in our own time by a brief study of the development of the monastic ideal—of men who went into the desert to seek God.

I

The Meaning of Monasticism

WHAT is the meaning of the monastic life? In some quarters it is taken for granted as an integral, permanent element in the life of the Church. In others the whole idea is rejected as an outworn superstition, abandoned once for all at the Reformation. Yet the fact remains that outside Protestantism, both in the Roman Catholic and the Orthodox Churches the monastic life has gone on all through the centuries, in spite of many difficulties and upheavals. It has certainly fluctuated in intensity, and like any other living phenomenon it is constantly assuming fresh forms; but in many countries all over the world it was never more alive than at the present day. Indeed, it is only when we see monasticism as an act of living religion that we begin to understand its meaning.

Père Louis Bouyer explains very clearly what monasticism means. It is the 'search for God—that is the beginning and the end of monasticism'.[1] But it is not a vague search; it is a 'search' because it is the answer to a *call*: for 'the monastic vocation . . . presupposes that God is Someone who has revealed Himself to us by a word, Someone who has called us. And to respond to the monastic vocation is to respond to this Person. Suddenly we realised that this call was to ourselves. And we set out in search of Him who was calling,

[1] L. Bouyer, *The Meaning of the Monastic Life* (Burns and Oates), p. 88.

calling to Him in our turn, calling Him with an appeal into which we put our whole heart, our whole life.'[1]

Origins: The Desert and St Basil

Just as prayer is found in every people in some form or other, so the existence of some forms of monasticism outside Christianity (as in Buddhism or the Dead Sea Scrolls community in Judaism) show the dim longing of man for God. But in Europe the growth of monasticism was a purely Christian development.[2]

From the early days of the Church there had been certain monastic or 'ascetic' tendencies within its life. Thus monasticism did not suddenly spring up 'out of the blue'. As a movement, however, it dates from the beginning of the fourth century.

This was the moment when Constantine became sole Emperor of Rome, and the Christians were free to worship and live in peace. They had just emerged from a nightmare period of persecution which had lasted for ten years. This persecution had been all the more devastating because it came on the Church suddenly after a period of outward peace. During this forty years' respite many had become slack, while others had joined the Church for various motives. When the pressure was lifted (in 313) the Christians went wild with joy. Thousands of pagans flocked into the Church to be 'on the right side'. The result was that Christian men and women who had come through the previous ten years of persecution were horrified to see the faith for which they had suffered, and for which so many had died, being watered down.

[1] *Ibid.*, pp. 8-9.
[2] K. E. Kirk, *The Vision of God* (Longmans), pp. 491 ff., deals fully with the alleged pagan origin of Christian monasticism. He examines Reitzenstein's theory that 'monasticism evolved or crystallized out of a general doctrine of the supremacy of the "spiritual man in the Graeco-Roman world"' very thoroughly—and rejects it finally for lack of satisfying evidence.

They contrasted this time with the Early Church, which as an island in the sea of paganism had been naturally puritan. 'Its moral standards were lofty, its discipline vigorous, its demands upon the faithful exacting.'[1] Its heroes had been the martyrs. The Christians of that early period—when to be caught worshipping at the Eucharist might mean instant death—had believed that they were called to be faithful unto death. In his *Exhortation to the Martyrs*, Tertullian had been trying to encourage a group of men and women in prison under sentence of death. He had urged them to regard their prison as the place where they could become still more devoted to Christ, and leave everything for his sake: 'The prison does for the Christian what the desert did for the prophet . . . Let us drop the name of "prison" and call it a "place of retirement". Though the body is shut in, all doors are open to the spirit.'[2] Thus long before the days of persecution were over the very word 'martyr' (witness) could be applied to anyone who lived a life of self-sacrifice in the service of God and his fellow-men. Bouyer lays great stress upon this point: 'Here we come to the final and also the fundamental idea of monasticism, the sole justification for its appearance in the history of the Christian Church; this idea is that monasticism and martyrdom . . . are but one and the same thing.'[3]

It is not surprising that men and women reared in this stern school should have felt uneasy and troubled in the changed atmosphere of the fourth century. They knew that in the earlier days Christians had often gone into the desert, sometimes under stress of persecution, sometimes simply to be alone and to pray. Now that life had outwardly become too easy, once more instinctively, the most earnest and devoted Christians fled into the desert. For they were afraid that if they did not get away and 'seek God' for themselves,

[1] *Western Asceticism* (Library of Christian Classics, SCM Press, vol. xii), ed. O. Chadwick, p. 13.   [2] *Ibid.*
[3] *The Meaning of the Monastic Life*, p. 54.

they would suffer from spiritual suffocation. They feared mediocrity, compromise, the lot of the half-hearted, the double-minded, the people who try to 'serve two masters': God and the world. They feared it like the devil, and that is why they fought it with such terrifying vigour. They did not spend their time criticizing others, but they set about trying to conquer the evil in themselves. They had fled into the desert to 'see God'; they sought him by prolonged and ardent prayer; after many trials they found him they sought. Joy broke out 'and the deserts of either side of the Nile re-echoed to the singing of the Psalms'.

Two names stand out in this first period of monasticism: St Anthony (251-356) and St Pachomius (290-346).

As a young man St Anthony of Egypt heard the call of Christ to 'leave all and follow'. He took this literally, sold his possessions and went into the desert for twenty years. There he endured great trials and temptations. About 305 he came out of his solitude to gather a few disciples into a kind of community with a common rule. He had been away for so long that his name had become a legend, and men flocked to see him. They expected a haggard, eccentric man, but instead they saw a perfectly normal, sane person, with an amazing personal influence. For some years he lived with his brethren until once more he felt the call to solitude. He stayed away for a long time. Towards the end of his life he was urged to come out and help the other brethren who were meeting numbers of men who had flocked into the desert, owing to the increasing secularization of the Church. Anthony helped them all a great deal. He was gentle and humane. Canon Hannay sums him up thus: 'He must have been very great, because he was very good.'[1]

Under St Pachomius, the desert hermitage developed into the monastery. His origin was very different from that of St Anthony: he was the poor son of a pagan family.

[1] See J. O. Hannay, *The Spirit and Origin of Christian Monasticism* (Methuen).

While still young he was forced into the Imperial army. During this time the kindness and goodness of some Christian people to the recruits impressed him so much that as soon as he was free, he joined the Christian Church. Soon after that he went into the desert and put himself under training with an older hermit. He prayed and worked and became a disciplined man. Then one day—as the result of a vision—he began to build a small enclosure which was the first monastery. It happened so quietly that even when a number of men came to live in the enclosure no one had noticed what was going on. This first experiment was not very happy. The hermits did not understand his aim; they treated him rudely, and refused all discipline. Wisely he gave them their freedom. Later on a few other men came to him, and accepted his Rule and the obedience it entailed. Gradually more and more people came to the new monastery, till it became far too small. When Pachomius died there were nine monasteries for men, and two for women, already established under his Rule.[1]

St Basil the Great (c. 330-79), the next great figure, came from a leading Christian family in Cappadocia (Asia Minor). When he returned from the University of Athens after a brilliant career he was a conceited young man. But his elder sister, Macrina, made him listen as she pointed out the uselessness of intellectual gifts unless they were used in the service of God. At first he argued fiercely. But in the end, as he says, he 'woke up'. He saw that he must find a better use for his life, but he did not know what to do. Having heard about the monasteries in his own country and in other parts of the Middle East, he made a prolonged tour among them.

When he came back he was a changed man. He was now 28, and he determined to become a monk. So he established a small monastery in beautiful mountain country, not far from his home. Under his guidance the monastic life began to develop in a new direction.

[1] See Helen Waddell, *The Desert Fathers* (Constable).

When he died in 379 the monastic life had been re-ordered in such a way that there was little of the primitive element left. Instead of groups of hermits, very loosely connected with one another, were several small, closely knit communities, each with its own head. The monastic movement was now based on the principle of community, but not on the semi-military organization of Pachomius; rather, Basil's idea was that of the Christian family, in which the members are bound together by love, and then seek to serve their neighbours by acts of love. Basil had a very active 'social conscience', so his monks not only did all the necessary manual work, but wherever possible they cared for the sick and helpless, fed the hungry and taught the children. One feature of this new kind of monasticism was the part taken in it by women. There were several double monasteries—a feature which was to recur later on.

The aim of the monastic life was the same: the priority of solitude, prayer, common worship, the use of the Bible and especially of the Psalms. One element had been added, for St Basil and his two colleagues were great theologians, highly educated in literature. Naturally many of the new monks came from the same kind of society, so the monastic movement now included culture and education. The primitive simplicity remained prominent in the development of monasticism in the Eastern Church, but it is not too much to say that the whole history of monasticism in the West has been influenced by St Basil's rich contribution.

St Benedict and Western Monasticism

Long before Rome fell in 410, Roman civilization had been dying. Cyprian, the Bishop of Carthage who was martyred in 258, wrote: 'The world itself now bears witness to its approaching end by its failing powers. . . . Can anything that is old preserve the same powers that it had in the prime and vigour of youth?' A Bishop of Lyons, writing at the beginning of the fifth century, speaks of a 'white-haired world', full of 'famine, plague, devastation, wars and terror'.

The fall of Rome was a world-shattering event. To Jerome it seemed that 'the light of the world was put out and the head of the Empire cut off'. For nearly six hundred years the Roman Empire had held out against the Barbarians who were massing on her frontiers. Towards the end of the fourth century the defences began to break down, and the Barbarians poured into the Empire, bringing death and destruction wherever they went. 'For twenty years and more', Jerome laments in 396, 'Roman blood has been flowing over broad countries between Constantinople and the Julian Alps. . . . Bishops live in prison, priests and clerics fall by the sword, churches are plundered, Christ's altars are turned into feeding-troughs. . . . On every side sorrow, on every side lamentation, everywhere the image of death.'

It was in this age that St Augustine lived and worked. He himself, at the time of his conversion, had been deeply impressed by the story of St Anthony. Later, when he became Bishop of Hippo, he formed a kind of clerical monastery which foreshadowed Western monasticism in its outlook. It was during the later part of his life, when the Barbarian terror was carrying all before it, that he wrote the *City of God*. When he died in 430, the monastic life was sweeping over Western Europe.

The ideals of Egyptian monasticism had been brought to Rome by Athanasius in 339. Owing to the disturbed state of the country many educated Christians fled to Gaul, and in particular to Provence. There several monasteries were founded. The most famous one was on the little island of Lérins (near Cannes). Here the spirit of the Desert Fathers was mediated through the writings of John Cassian. He did more than this : through the medium of his thought and experience, he transmitted an ideal of monasticism which contained not only the primitive element but also the later elements which came through Origen and St Basil. He thus became the great source of inspiration for the monastic life of the West. Through all his writings the aim of monasticism stands out in clear relief: it is 'to cleave to God himself', to be instant in prayer—a prayer which is wholly set upon God.

These monasteries in southern Gaul had a great influence. At Lérins in particular there was a great influx of men from different countries. The little islands in the neighbourhood (till then uninhabited) soon became full of hermits and contemplative monks: 'seekers after God', as they were described by St Hilary of Arles. From Lérins and this region there went out a spirit which profoundly affected the life of the Western world—first of all through the very fact that here the way to God was kept open night and day by ceaseless worship, offered to him in silence and solitude; secondly, because out of this life came men who were to be the bishops and apostles of a Church yet to be born. It is even possible that St Patrick spent some time there, while he was preparing for his future work as the Apostle of Ireland—a land which later became known as the Isle of Saints, and the centre of Celtic monasticism.

As the years passed, however, the first freshness wore off and the monastic movement became confused and sporadic. For Anthony, Basil and Cassian, the Vision of God was the supreme aim of the monastic life. But in a confused situation many monasteries lost sight of this aim; then they began to be more occupied with straining after an 'experience': watching *themselves*, instead of looking up to God. The lack of a central organization was an added difficulty. There were so many different 'rules' and customs that some monasteries were fervent and ascetic to a fanatical degree, while others were slack and careless, and were 'monasteries' only in name. Many monks were for ever changing monasteries as the whim took them, and wandering about all over the countryside.

It was the destiny of one man to bring order and sanity

into this confused and dangerous situation: Benedict of Nursia (c. 480-550). We know very little about his life, but his name shines with a bright and steadfast light out of the darkness of those ages of misery, terror and destruction. He lived in an Italy wholly overshadowed by the inroads of the Goths and Huns. Their constant raids and pillage caused the breakdown of social order, and an almost continual state of famine.

As a young man Benedict went to Rome for further study, but the degeneracy and godlessness he saw there repelled him so violently that he fled from the city and took refuge in a cave where he remained for a long while alone, praying and thinking. Eventually some wandering monks discovered him. They made friends with him, and finally the best of them asked him to train them for a purer monastic life. He formed them into small communities of twelve, each with its own abbot. Soon there were twelve of these small communities. For various reasons he left his former dwelling and founded his great Abbey on Monte Cassino.

All that St Benedict was and sought may be gathered from his famous Rule, which was gradually accepted as the standard of monastic life in the West. As we read it we can see that he was a very wise, compassionate, dedicated man. For the first time in the history of the Church, he drew up a rule which a normal human being could accept.

The monk's day was divided into three periods: for worship, work and rest. The monks were to live very simply, but were not to injure their health by extremes of fasting or lack of sleep. In many ways, so far as externals were concerned, probably the day of a Benedictine monk was not very different from that of most working men outside. Great stress was laid upon work. But the fundamental aim of the monastic life is clearly stated: the monastery is to be 'a school of the Lord's service'. Every new recruit is to be examined carefully on this one point: does he seek God? Now 'to seek God' might be simply a pious phrase. But for

St Benedict as for all other great monastic leaders, it had a profound meaning. It was the reiteration of the primitive ideal to seek God only, without any compromise; to follow Christ without question—even to death. Later on many Benedictine monks became social reformers, scholars or statesmen; but this was not the purpose of their Rule. All that Benedict aimed at was that they should be good men. He left the question of their usefulness to God.

So in the midst of destruction and disorder the Rule of St Benedict held up a practicable idea of creative ordered life.

In the words of Cardinal Newman, 'St Benedict found the world, physical and social, in ruins, and his mission was to restore it, in the way not of science but of nature, not as if setting about to do it, not professing to do it by any set time, or by any rare specific, but so quietly, patiently, gradually, that often till the work was done it was not known to be doing. It was a restoration rather than a visitation, correction, or conversion. The new work which he helped to create was a growth rather than a structure. Silent men were observed about the country, or discovered in the forest digging, clearing and building; and other silent men, not seen, were sitting in the cold cloister, tiring their eyes and keeping their attention on the stretch, while they painfully copied and recopied the manuscripts which they had saved. There was no one who contended or cried out or drew attention to what was going on, but by degrees the woody swamp became a hermitage, a religious house, a farm, an abbey, a village, a seminary, a school of learning, and a city.'[1]

The 'Dark Ages' began about the year 400 and lasted— with one interval of fifty years—until about 1000. It was a period of appalling horror, violence, moral decay, social distress and confusion. 'It was a night in which humanity seemed to be groping blindly amid the bloody confusion of

[1] Quoted by C. Dawson in *Religion and the Rise of Western Culture* (Sheed and Ward), p. 58.

to-day and the anguish of the morrow.'[1] Yet during this period there was a great expansion of monastic life, almost entirely on the Benedictine model. The influence of these monasteries—when they remained true to their vocation—was outstanding; they were the centres of deep spiritual life, which overflowed in missionary zeal and compassionate service to the hungry and the suffering. They were havens of intellectual life, preserving some remnants of culture in the midst of war and violence. In addition, by their very industry and common sense they were the pioneers, almost unconsciously, of a better social life for thousands.

Despite such achievements, the monasteries themselves were often involved in the darkness. An episcopal report drawn up at Troslé in 909 declares that 'the cities are depopulated, the monasteries ruined and burned, the land is reduced to a solitude . . .' The bishops themselves are accused. 'It has come about by our negligence, our ignorance, and that of our brethren, that there is in the Church a multitude of both sexes who . . . are ignorant even of the words of the Creed and the Lord's Prayer.'[2]

Efforts at monastic reform were all gathered up in one mighty effort by the famous Abbey of Cluny in Burgundy, founded in 910. The new movement began very quietly with the appointment of St Berno at the head of a small group of twelve Benedictine monks. For the next two hundred years this Abbey was ruled by a succession of saintly and progressive abbots. St Odo, abbot 927-42, began by returning to the first principles of St Benedict, centering the whole monastic life upon the *Opus Dei*, the work of God. As time went on the numbers increased and Cluniac monks led an exemplary life. When we remember the state of 'civilization' at that time, it is something of a shock to find that St Odo insisted on extreme cleanliness, and even provided wash-basins and towels.

[1] H. Daniel-Rops, *The Church in the Dark Ages* (Dent), p. 246.
[2] C. Dawson, *Religion and the Rise of Western Culture*, pp. 143-7.

This reform movement spread quickly. By the year 1100 or so there were nearly a thousand monasteries affiliated to Cluny, scattered over France, Germany, Spain, Italy and Britain. This was no mere outward achievement, it was a true reform, or better still, a 'renewal' of religious life. 'True reform', says H. Daniel-Rops, 'had to come from the Church herself, through a break between her and feudal society. The monks of Cluny understood this, and what they did was nothing short of revolutionary.' But the influence of Cluny was not external or violent, it was 'intensive, silent and profound'.[1]

As time went on, however, although Cluny had many saints in its ranks, even here the standard of 'perfection' was unconsciously lowered. Over-activity of one kind and another tended to crowd out the 'one thing needful'. During the eleventh and twelfth centuries many efforts were made to reform the monastic life. These reformers were in continual protest against the corruption of the Church and the prevalence of simony. One of these reformers was St Bruno (1032-1101). Having made a violent protest against the scandals in his own diocese he turned his back on the world and sought absolute solitude. He found it in the mountains above Grenoble. In 1084, in an almost inaccessible spot, with a few companions he founded the Grande Chartreuse. This monastery was unique in the fact that it combined both the solitary and the communal life. Bruno did not intend to found an Order. But some years later, the Pope approved the 'customs' of the Carthusians and they became an Order. Although this Order has had to suffer much from external events, in itself it has never needed 'reform'. It has remained true to its vocation 'to seek God' only. Living in the light of eternity it has preserved the joy of its youth.

The Carthusian life was—and is—one of great austerity, with much silence and solitude. Yet the Order spread gradually all over Europe. One of the most famous Carthusians in

[1] *The Church in the Dark Ages*, p. 581.

England was St Hugh, Bishop of Lincoln (d. 1200). He was the son of a Burgundian noble. At the age of 19, when he had been ordained deacon, he was filled with the desire to join the Grande Chartreuse, 'built almost above the clouds, and very near to God'. His superiors were not willing to part with him, but at length they consented. In 1160 he entered the Chartreuse where he served faithfully and joyfully for ten years. Later his prior sent him to England to build up a small 'charterhouse' at Witham in Somerset. Finally in 1186, the King (Henry II) insisted on having Hugh made Bishop of Lincoln. There he lived an exemplary life and was greatly loved. He gave away the deer in his parks to feed the poor, improved the state of the clergy, opposed the King wherever he saw injustice and oppression. His biographer tells us that he loved not only animals, but 'children and even babies'.

A few years after the foundation of the Grande Chartreuse a new Order was founded in 1098 at Cîteaux near Dijon. This ushered in a great monastic revival, the most important of the twelfth century. This period, usually regarded as the golden age of medieval monasticism, was shot through by a sense of crisis and imminent judgment. Reform and a longing for renewal were in the air. In the middle of that century a German ecclesiastic gathered up his deep concern for the Church in the following prayer :

Come then, Lord Jesus, come to thy ship, the Holy Church, which is labouring heavily in this fourth watch of the night : come, O Lord, rule in the midst of thine enemies, the false priests who sell and rob in thine house, and the princes who tyrannize in the name of Christ. Come, Saviour Jesus, working salvation in the midst of the earth, and the midst of the Church making peace between the Kingdom and the priesthood.[1]

[1] C. Dawson, *Religion and the Rise of Western Culture*, p. 248. See also Louis Bouyer, *The Cistercian Heritage* (Mowbray).

Historians used to suggest that the immediate cause of this break-away from Cluny was the decadence of that Order. Now, however, the strange fact emerges that this move took place when Cluny was still at the height of its power. These new monks went to Cîteaux, to start a new order, for a very different reason : they went there because they desired something Cluny could not give them.

The Cluniac Reform, when it was 'new', was based upon a return to the Rule of St Benedict and the spirit of primitive monasticism. The Cistercians, who now were 'new', wanted to do exactly the same. They wanted to live in the pure spirit of the Rule of St Benedict. They claimed that Cluny had developed into something so different that they longed for the purer air of the earliest ages of monasticism. They interpreted the Rule of St Benedict itself in the light of the teaching of the Desert Fathers, mediated through the writings of Cassian. In so doing they were in line with the outlook of their own day.

Many forms of religious life were now looking back to the primitive period. At first the reform went slowly. Then came the sudden brilliance of Cîteaux, due to the arrival of St Bernard, in 1112, with some thirty relatives and friends. It was Bernard who put Cîteaux on the map. Indeed, almost all its initial success and influence was due to his amazing leadership. He was a European figure and yet a true father to his monks. To him, and his companions, the aim of the Cistercian reform was a great deal more than the literal observance of the Benedictine Rule : it was simply 'to seek God' in contemplation, and live their whole life to his glory.

For a time the new Order flourished exceedingly, both inwardly and outwardly. But by 1250 or so there were signs of decline. The Black Death and the Hundred Years' War affected it profoundly. But these events were not the cause of its decline : that had been at work secretly for a long time. This was due in part to the very virtues of the Cistercian Order : the monks had gone into trade, with such success that their monasteries had become wealthy. They had to market great supplies of wheat and wine and oil and wool. They had to do business on a large scale, with large warehouses and commercial agencies. Monks had to make long journeys for business purposes; some, for instance, had to travel on river boats to ship cargoes of wine from the Moselle down the Rhine to Holland. The result was that though these men continued to lead exemplary lives, and used their riches to help the poor and the sick, they became so busy and active that the spirit of prayer evaporated. The body was still there, 'doing good', but the spirit had gone out of it.

The Canons Regular and the Friars

Alongside of this constant effort at 'reformation' in the monastic life, there was another, equally important, sphere in which reform was urgently needed: in the life of the clergy.

This problem had exercised the minds of many Popes and religious leaders, but matters came to a head in the twelfth century. While the Cluniac movement was setting itself to reform the monasteries, another movement arose in Lorraine which aimed at reforming the life of the clergy, especially of the priests attached to cathedrals and large churches. This reform was based upon the renewal of the communal life for the clergy, or the 'canonical' life. Both in England and on the Continent those who adhered to this reform were known as 'Austin Canons' because they were living by a Rule called the Rule of St Augustine. This was generally accepted as coming from St Augustine himself, since it was well known that he had established the communal life for the clergy in his own diocese. Indeed, 'this clerical monastery at Hippo represents a turning-point in the history of monasticism. Instead of fleeing from the world, it turned its face towards the world'.[1]

[1] W. Nigg, *Warriors of God*, pp. 106 ff.

These canons were called 'Canons Regular'. They lived in community under their bishop, observed a strict Rule, and laid great emphasis on prayer, silence and self-denial. This was the heart of their life and it enabled them to go out into the world around them as preachers and pastors in the district or diocese to which they belonged.

One of the most famous leaders of this movement was St Norbert of Xanten, near Cologne in the Rhineland, where he was born in 1080. He was of high birth (his name means 'Prince of the North') and well educated. Following the lax practices of the time he was given a good benefice, and indeed was a cathedral canon before he was ordained to the priesthood. Then, at the age of nineteen, this young man was suddenly converted. He went away into a desert place, to think and to pray. Being a man who tended to go to extremes, after a time he came back to his fellows and tried to convert them. Great was the indignation of the comfortable clerics. So Norbert left them, and became a wandering preacher. Finally, on the suggestion of the Pope (for by this time Norbert was well known), he settled down in a forest near Laon, and founded a house of 'Canons Regular' at a place called Prémontré. This house attracted many serious priests. In 1126 the Pope made Norbert Archbishop of Magdeburg.

The movement grew till the Premonstratensian Canons were known all over Western Europe. They did a great deal of missionary work, especially in the neglected Slavonic countries beyond the Elbe. In 1339 the houses which followed the Rule of St Augustine were gathered together by the Pope and constituted an Order. By 1350, this Order had 1,300 houses in Western Europe.

The coming of the Friars was like a breath of spring after a long, stormy winter. To use the words of Chesterton, it was from St Francis of Assisi (1182-1226) that there came 'a whole awakening of the world and a dawn in which all shapes and colours could be seen anew'. During the Dark Ages a certain kind of order *had* been emerging out of chaos; and now, when prophetic voices were announcing the coming of a new Age, 'a figure appeared silently and suddenly on a little hill . . . dark against the fading darkness. For it was the end of a long stern night not unvisited by stars. He stood with his hands lifted . . . and about him was a burst of birds singing, and behind him was the break of day.'[1]

We all know the story of St Francis: how the light of Christ first dawned on his own soul, how he threw everything over, all his youthful hopes and dreams—in order to follow Christ absolutely. In his short life he became, and has remained ever since, a 'splendid and merciful mirror of Christ'. Umbria was his Galilee and Mount Alvernia his Calvary. He brought new energy to the life of the Western Church. And he did this in great simplicity, because he followed the Gospel, and what he gave to his disciples was a way of life, not a code.

Very early in his new career, Francis was joined by St Clare, a girl of noble birth and great force of character. After the first agitation—in her family—over her unconventional escape into a new form of religious life, she was enabled to settle down at San Damiano (close to Assisi) in a small poor convent of which she became the first abbess. She and her sisters were a great encouragement to the new order, and to St Francis himself, as they lived and prayed in their little home on the hill.

As time went on, there arose, quite naturally, an informal society composed of people who wanted to lead a new life on Franciscan principles. They came from all classes and groups in the life of that day: men and women, married and single, rich and poor, educated and ignorant. Most of these Tertiaries went on living in their own homes and carried on

[1] G. K. Chesterton, *St Francis of Assisi* (Hodder and Stoughton), p. 39.

their daily work; but some retired from the world, spent much time in prayer and in the service of the sick and suffering. Others gave away most of their possessions. In whatever way they interpreted their call, their Rule enabled them to challenge the accepted standards of the day. For instance, 'poverty' for most of them (if they were not poor already) meant a life of simplicity, challenging the increasing love of luxury and pleasure. They were 'not to carry arms', which meant that they were not to take part in feuds, or intervene in warfare, whether the cause were 'just' or not. They were 'men of peace', and all of them—men and women alike—tried to 'live according to the Gospel', to pray, and to love their neighbours, and to make peace wherever they could; while all of them did all in their power to help and to succour the outcasts, the poor and the helpless, nursing the sick and caring for lepers. Thus the message of St Francis was for all men.

St Dominic (1170-1221), the founder of the other great Order of Friars, has not made the same impression on the popular imagination, but his influence has been, and still is, very great.[1] He has not left much in the way of spiritual writings, but his contemporaries speak of his austerity, of his exquisite charity, of the 'nights spent in prayer, and the spiritual power that radiated from and even seemed to inform his physical frame'. It is an interesting fact that an early biographer tells us that St Dominic fed his mind and heart by constant reading and re-reading the *Conferences* of John Cassian. Thus we see the aim of monasticism carried out in another form so many centuries later.

Dominic's constant prayer was that he 'might have a true love of souls and ability to help others'. In these two indications we see the germ of the twofold character of his Order : it was to be both monastic and apostolic.

Dominic was the son of a Castilian noble, full of fiery

[1] See David Knowles, *The Religious Orders in England*, vol. i, part 2 (Cambridge).

Spanish zeal. Intended for the Church, he spent several years at the University of Palencia (in Leon); then he became a Canon Regular at Osma, and a close friend of the bishop, Dom Diego. Dominic soon made his mark as a great preacher; people listened to him spellbound, for they said, 'it seemed as though God were speaking through him'. He was full of missionary zeal and longed to go to 'foreign countries' to preach the Gospel, but when he asked the Pope to sanction his ideas the Pope said, 'Why go so far? Surely the field lies at your door in Languedoc where these heretics are leading so many people astray!' So Dominic joined a large group of men who had been sent on this mission: to try to convert the large and growing sect of the Cathari (or Albigenses) who swarmed in Provence. They have been described by a modern Dominican as 'the Communists of the thirteenth century'. The growth of heresy was due to the increasing interest of lay folk in religion, and their indignation at the low state of the Church, especially among the clergy.

Dominic's first effort at 'converting' these people was not successful. He retired to Osma for a time and reflected upon the reason. He then saw that his approach should be quite different. On his second visit the inhabitants of the towns and villages were startled by the appearance of Dominic and his friends. They came very quietly and humbly, dressed in poor clothes, and indeed, as the people said, with wonder, they were just like their own leaders, 'the Perfect': modest and charitable and accessible to everyone. Everywhere the missionaries went they had a good hearing, and several of the Cathari came back to the Church. When Dominic saw that the missionary movement was well under way he decided that he must leave it in other hands for a time. But his first act before leaving Provence was to establish a community of women in a little town near the Pyrenees; he felt that the work of women at prayer was most important.

Unfortunately, the peaceful campaign of preaching and

teaching was suddenly broken off in 1208 by the murder of the Papal legate. This led to the terrible crusade against the 'heretics' under Simon de Montfort. Dominic took no part in this campaign; it was against all his principles. Meanwhile, he was gathering Brothers round him and they were becoming aware of their common vocation. With the Pope's warm approval the Order of Preachers was constituted in January 1217.

The first Brothers were a mere handful of sixteen: Spaniards, Normans, English, French, Provençal, Navarais, and some from Languedoc. Poverty was a necessary element in their Rule, for they wished to be free to serve God wherever they were needed. From the beginning, as men dedicated to preaching, it was seen that they must be both students and theologians. From the outset, they established themselves at three strategic points: the great universities of Rome, Paris and Bologna.

Once the initial task of organization had been well accomplished, St Dominic went on with his own task of travelling, teaching and preaching all over western Europe. When he finally returned, exhausted, to Bologna in July 1221, eight Dominican Provinces were already functioning; in Spain, Provence, Lombardy, Rome, Germany, England and Hungary. On 6th August he died in great peace.

The immense success of the Mendicant Orders (as the Friars were called, because they begged for their food) showed that they met an urgent need. They travelled everywhere; preached and taught in churches, convents, castles, as well as at tournaments and in the open air. Their appearance was simple, austere and poor. In some ways they were like the early Methodists or the Salvation Army. Everywhere they spoke out plainly and fearlessly in the language of the people. In 1223 the Franciscans and the Dominicans joined in a great effort at peace-making. This 'mission' had spectacular results in reconciliation between families, classes and

Iona

St Julian's

Lee Abbey

cities. They lived and spoke of God and holy things in a way which went to the hearts of people, young and old, rich and poor, learned and uneducated. As time went on their work became more and more varied : it was social and pastoral as well as missionary. They cared for sick people and lepers, and in all epidemics of plague they were to the fore in the care of the sick and the dying. As their Orders grew so their mission went further afield : the Dominicans to the great universities, and the Franciscans to missions in Eastern Europe, India and China.

But as years passed, even these successful movements could not stem the tide of worldliness within the Church. The tide ebbed and flowed; reform succeeded reform, and still great evils flourished. Some far more drastic change was now required. Karl Adam, a modern Catholic writer, says about his own country in the late fifteenth century : 'Night fell on the German Church, a night that grew even darker and darker.' This was true of most of Western Christendom : 'among the common people a fearful decline of true piety into religious materialism and morbid hysteria; amongst the clergy, both lower and higher, widespread worldliness and neglect of duty; and amongst the very shepherds of the Church, demoniac ambition and sacrilegious perversion of holy things. Both clergy and people must cry *mea culpa, mea maxima culpa.*'[1]

From the Reformation to the Revolution

'Night fell.' By 1541 the unity of Christendom—such as it was—had been shattered; the fragmented sections continued to live and develop in separation, with unhappy results on both sides.

Once the Protestant Reformation had taken place, the Roman Catholic Church set about the task of reform within her own borders. This she did at the highest level through the Council of Trent (1545-63), which defined and codified

[1] Karl Adam, *One and Holy* (Sheed and Ward), pp. 23, 25.

B

doctrine, emphasized the spiritual and pastoral significance of the office of bishop, and decided to establish better training for the clergy.

Behind this external reform movement, however, lay a hidden movement of prayer, working chiefly through small groups which met in private, read and discussed the Bible together, and prayed for the purification of the Church beginning with themselves. One of these groups used to meet in a small church in Rome between 1510 and 1520. Its members were priests and laymen, solid citizens and intellectuals. Their chief aim was to 'reform themselves'. 'The fact that at the very origin of the great movement of Catholic renewal prayer had the first place is a fact of profound significance.'[1]

The first great instrument of the renewal or Counter-Reformation was the creation of a new Order. For a great leader emerged who gathered up in himself the seething aspirations of so many who longed for a religious advance. Ignatius Loyola (1491-1556), the founder of the Society of Jesus (the Jesuits), was the man of the hour. His Order was new, yet in principle it did not break with the great Orders of the past, which still survived though they were often in great need of reform and new life. The aim of this new Order was to be at the absolute disposal of God and the Church : to go anywhere, to do anything, in order that the Christian faith might be carried all over the world.

Special emphasis was laid upon the virtue of obedience. The Jesuit monks wore no special habit, nor did they use the regular choir offices. The life of the Order was based upon prayer : *The Spiritual Exercises of St Ignatius* were written to enable candidates for membership of the Order to find out, in a prolonged retreat, whether they had a vocation to this particular way of life, which would enable them to stand it. This book has had a great influence, far beyond its original purpose. The Jesuits were very well trained. They

[1] H. Daniel-Rops, *The Catholic Reformation* (Dent), p. 10.

have always been a great force in education. But none of their great achievements would have been possible had they not been from the outset a compact body of men, filled with fiery zeal for the Kingdom of God, disciplined in life and thought, ready to do and dare for the sake of the Gospel.

When Ignatius died in 1556 it is said that there were already a thousand members of the Order. This was probably the strongest missionary movement since the days of the apostles. The name of St Francis Xavier stands out among these devoted men, for he went through Asia like a flame. In the words of Macaulay: 'The Jesuits invaded all the countries which the great maritime discoveries of the preceding age had laid open to European enterprise. They were to be found in the depths of Peruvian mines, at the marts of African slave caravans, on the shores of the Spice Islands, in the observatories of China.'[1]

Spain produced another reforming movement of the greatest importance: the Carmelite Reform led by St Teresa of Avila (1515-82) and St John of the Cross (1542-91).

During the closing stages of the Council of Trent, in 1562, in a little town in Old Castile, something happened which seemed insignificant at the time, but was destined to be the beginning of far-reaching reform. In the heart of the ancient town of Avila the inhabitants heard the tinkling of a bell from a new, small convent. On that hot August day, in obedience to a call from God, Teresa stepped out of the conventional religious world in which she had been living, in order to lead a life of utter devotion, self-denial and poverty. This act of hers was like a seed which grew into a great tree, for out of her life the reformed Carmelite Order spread to many countries, and is still blessing the world today.

Teresa's desire to reform the Carmelite Order, and restore it to a life of solitude, silence, poverty and deep contempla-

[1] Father James Brodrick has written biographies of *St Ignatius Loyola* and *St Francis Xavier* (Burns and Oates).

tion—in other words, to renounce mediocrity and aim at holiness—was accompanied by a great desire to be 'apostles of prayer', interceding for the salvation of the world.

St Teresa stands in the great succession of women saints, like St Hildegarde of Bingen, St Catherine of Siena and St Catherine of Genoa. It was because she knew in her own experience the misery of a 'double-minded life' that she struck out on a new life of consecration and reform. Her influence was great in her own day, and it has continued down to the present time.[1]

Thus the first movements of reform came from Italy and Spain. But in the seventeenth century France took the lead. An outstanding figure in this era was St Vincent de Paul (1576-1660), whose wisdom and compassion were constantly creating new 'works of mercy' : for prisoners and slaves, for the sick and suffering, for the hungry and the destitute. The Church, too, was quickened by his genius : in better theological training for priests, and in many other ways which bore lasting fruit.

At the same time there was a revival of monastic life. Numbers of new Orders were founded, and this at a time when a great many of the older monasteries and convents had fallen so low that their laxity and immorality were a by-word. One of the outstanding figures in this movement is St Francis de Sales (1567-1622), that saintly man who, it was said, had 'brought religion out of the cloister into the world'. Although he helped Madame de Chantal (1572-1641) to found the new Order for women—the Order of the Visitation—his first idea was that the Sisters should go out into the world and help to care for the sick and needy. It was only after a great deal of resistance on the part of the more conservative elements in the Church that he agreed that this Order should be 'enclosed'. His famous book, *An Introduction to the Devout Life*, had a fantastic reception in his lifetime, and translations into other languages have been ap-

[1] See E. Allison Peers, *Mother of Carmel* (SCM Press).

pearing ever since. He showed that it was possible for ordinary people to live a fully Christian life in the world.

But this creative period—in music, painting, literature, as well as in religion—came to an end about 1660. A new chapter began in the history of France and of the world, at the moment when the young Louis XIV at the death of Mazarin announced 'I will be my own Prime Minister'. It was also a new chapter in the history of the Church. M. Vincent died in 1660, Pascal in 1662, and many other great men died soon afterwards. The leaders had disappeared. The life of the court was scandalous in the extreme, not only in France, but also in Spain. Philip IV, the 'most Catholic King', had 32 natural children. The state of many monasteries was also very bad. It is a paradox that the age of Bossuet, Fénelon, Bourdaloue, de Rancé and de la Salle was also an age of decadence. The period of enthusiasm was over. The Christian leaders were there, it is true, and they went on with courage, but much of the good they might have done was frustrated by bitter controversies among themselves. This weakened the life of the Church, and opened the way for the triumph of intolerance on the one hand and scepticism on the other. The Church was in no fit state to meet the storms of the eighteenth century.

Many 'advanced' thinkers were now openly hostile to Christianity. After 1770 the successors of Voltaire were no longer deists but atheists. And the weakness of the Church was becoming increasingly evident : love of money and luxury among the hierarchy, competition for wealthy dioceses, prelates who were often absentees and lived at court. One cardinal died in 1741 without ever having entered the diocese to which he had been assigned twenty years before. When Louis XVI objected to a certain bishop being appointed Archbishop of Paris he said frankly : 'The Archbishop of Paris ought at least to believe in God!' It was the same among the clergy. The theological seminaries had lost their meaning; the students were wild and undisciplined.

Crime was rampant, and brutality widespread. While the misery of the poor was obvious, the springs of compassion were drying up. There were fewer hospitals and hospices than there had been in the previous century. This situation was as bad in Italy, Germany and Bohemia as in France.

It was like hearing the walls of an old house cracking before the final collapse. Many of the Religious Orders were involved in this decline. The suppression of the Jesuit Order in 1773 was a sign of the times. Voltaire exclaimed: 'In twenty years the Church will have disappeared altogether'.

By the end of the reign of Louis XVI it was obvious that revolution was imminent. The fact that the Church authorities were hand-in-glove with the oppressive and ineffective government naturally meant that it was totally involved in the catastrophe. Some historians maintain that at this moment the Church of France was at a lower ebb than it had ever been since the Christian faith first came to Gaul.

Yet, in spite of this gloomy situation, the threatened complete breakdown of the Church did not take place. Less than twenty years after Voltaire's hopeful prediction a large number of Christian men and women died for the faith during the Revolution. In 1789, it is true, there were far too many worldly bishops, but between 1792 and 1795 several died rather than desert their flocks. There were far too many irreligious priests, but there were several who risked their lives as 'chaplains of the guillotine'; and many others who all through the terror refused to take the oath, knowing what risks they ran. Some nuns were unfaithful to their vocation, but there were many who were the very opposite: for instance, the famous Sixteen Carmelites of Compiègne who went firmly to the scaffold, singing the *Te Deum* to the last.[1]

The wave of revolution swept over many countries of Western Europe, but when the tide receded it was clear that the Church had not been swept away.

[1] See the play by Georges Bernanos, *The Carmelites* (now translated in Fontana Books).

2

Community Life in the British Isles

MONASTIC life was established in Britain at a very early date. For some centuries Celtic monasticism in Ireland and Scotland was a vital religious force. The Church in Britain owes a great debt to the influence of St Patrick and St Columba. When the Latin form of monastic life came to England it soon took root, and became a great tree. The ruins of the great abbeys, where regular worship was offered for hundreds of years, are a reminder of those days. The causes which led to the collapse of monasticism in Britain were the same as those on the Continent.[1]

In the main, the suppression of the English monasteries was accepted fairly quietly. In itself it was the natural outcome of the new outlook which was affecting the court and the universities. The monks did not count; even the man-in-the-street asked pertinently : 'Why should they be supported at vast expense?' Most of them were given pensions. Some became clergymen in the Church of England; some even became bishops. Many were quite glad to be free to seek other work and to lead a freer life. About 5,000 monks, 1,600 friars and 2,000 nuns were thus pensioned off.

But there were those who did care : the saints and idealists. These were the true sufferers, for these were the monks

[1] The standard modern survey is by Professor David Knowles, *The Monastic Order in England* and *The Religious Orders in England*, 3 vols. (Cambridge).

who strove to realize the ideal of religious life, the life of men who dedicate themselves to prayer for sinful and suffering mankind. These men, who were hanged at Tyburn or at their abbey gates, were the martyrs. Some were heroic, some were weak, but all went through much bewilderment and pain: 'Brethren, this is a parlous time. . . . Such a scourge was never heard sith Christ's Passion.'[1]

By 1540 the English medieval monasteries had disappeared, and for the next three hundred years (with one brief exception) there were no religious Orders in England outside the Roman Catholic minority. The English reformers agreed with the Continental reformers in rejecting the monastic ideal. Their views are well represented in this statement from the appendix to the Augsburg Confession:

What is taught among us on the subject of monastic vows will be better understood if the state of the monasteries is considered, and how many things contrary to the canons were daily done in them. At the time of Augustine they were free colleges. Afterwards, when discipline became corrupt, vows were everywhere added, so that by a type of imprisonment discipline might be restored.[2]

This statement is important because, although it rejects medieval monasticism, it recognizes that there have been other forms of monasticism which were less objectionable. This leaves the way open for a wider and more profound understanding of the meaning of the monastic life and its place within the structure of the Church as a whole.

By the seventeenth century in England, however, there was a change of view within the Church of England. Here they did not agree entirely with the continental Reformers.

[1] Sir Maurice Powicke, *The Reformation in England* (Oxford), p. 34.
[2] B. J. Kidd, *Documents . . . of the Continental Reformation* (Oxford), p. 279.

For instance, Lancelot Andrewes wrote: 'Nor was it the King's intention to condemn the original foundations of monasticism, but rather the monks who have long since fallen from that foundation'. Archbishop Bramhall, writing in 1654, says plainly: 'We believe that foundations which were good in their original institution ought not to be destroyed for accessory abuses, or for the faults of particular persons.' The whole subject is treated with greater fulness by Herbert Thorndike (1598-1672), who asserts that 'the monastic life, if not of the *esse* (essence) of the Church, is at least of its fulness and perfection'. He adds: 'Seeing it is a perfection to Christianity, it is certainly a blot in the reformation which we profess that we are without it'. One of his repeated statements is important for the later development of Orders; he insists that the monastic community be private, and no part of the public, authorized, structure of the Church.[1]

In spite of various theoretical suggestions and practical efforts (such as that of Nicholas Ferrar's household at Little Gidding under Charles I, a very original 'family community'), when we look at the whole period from the Reformation to the beginning of the nineteenth century we have to admit that the general outlook of the Church of England was strongly against monasticism in general, and that most people knew very little about either its history or its meaning. Nevertheless, there were some who understood and valued the 'religious life'. Chief among them was William Law. In his *Serious Call to a Devout Life*, he says:

God may be served and glorified in every state of life, but as there are some states of life more desirable than others . . . so those who are at liberty to choose for themselves, seem to be called of God to be more eminently devoted to His service. Ever since the beginning of Christianity, there hath been two orders

[1] A. M. Allchin, *The Silent Rebellion: Anglican Religious Communities 1845-1900* (SCM Press), p. 18.

or ranks of People among good Christians. The one that feared and served God in the common offices and business of a secular worldly life. The other renouncing the common business and common enjoyments of life, as riches, marriage, honours and pleasure, devoted themselves to voluntary poverty, virginity, devotion and retirement, that by this means they might live wholly unto God, in the daily exercise of a divine and heavenly life.

The Anglican Revival

In the nineteenth century we come to the revival of the religious life, due to the Oxford Movement which developed into Anglo-Catholicism. This was not quite such an isolated phenomenon as has sometimes been thought. At this distance in time we can now see that it was deeply influenced by the strong Evangelical Movement of the early part of the nineteenth century. Indeed Bishop Frere said plainly, in his reflections on the revival of religious communities in this country, that 'in many ways it would be true to state that the Evangelical movement gave the spirit, and the Catholic movement the form, of this revival'.[1] At the same time, the Catholic influence was very strong. The leaders of the Oxford Movement were theologians. They looked back to, and reflected upon, the example of monasticism in the early Church and in the Middle Ages, and the life and the teaching of the religious Orders in the seventeenth century in France.

From 1845 onwards the Anglo-Catholics were a minority movement and the effort to found and develop religious communities had to be carried on very slowly and quietly, in the teeth of public opinion. But it had begun, and J. M. Neale, speaking in 1860, said with some exaggeration :

Twenty years ago the Religious Life was a ruin. Scarcely more in our Church than abroad. Everywhere the same. The spirit was lost; the outward laws of ritual were almost forgotten; even

[1] *English Church Ways* (1914), pp. 79-82.

on the Continent earnest men regarded vows and asceticism as things of the past. 'Son of man, can these dry bones live? And I said, Lord, Thou knowest.'[1]

What had happened in these twenty years? The Oxford Movement of 1833-45 was dominated by two convictions : (*a*) that the Church of England was identical with the Catholic Church in England, of earlier ages; (*b*) a belief in, and a longing for, true holiness, for a holiness which they believed that a true 'Catholicism' alone could produce.[2]

Père Louis Bouyer says that the greatness of the Oxford Movement 'was that it was neither a simply intellectual revival, nor like Methodism, a religious revival without doctrinal basis. The theological effort carried a spiritual renewal inescapably with it, just as the most authentic religious needs lay at the root of its speculative researches. . . . Their particular merit was that they recognized . . . *that there can be no Christian holiness save that which is founded on truth.*'[3]

The foundation of religious communities was the natural outcome of the Movement. Indeed the Movement's real meaning lies behind all the external controversies and conflicts, in the hidden life and development of the sisterhoods. For it was amongst women that the first communities were founded. The first Anglican Sister since the Reformation was a young girl, Marion Hughes. In Oxford on Trinity Sunday, 1841, she took the three vows of poverty, chastity and obedience, privately in the presence of Dr Pusey, and then went to St Mary's Church to receive Holy Communion at the hands of the vicar, J. H. Newman. She was 23. At the moment this action did not lead to the founding

[1] *Sermons Preached in a Religious House*, 2nd series (1874), vol. i, p. 306.

[2] Father Harold Ellis provides a simple account of this movement in *The Hand of the Lord* (Mirfield Publications).

[3] Quoted on pp. 53-4 of A. M. Allchin's *The Silent Rebellion*, to which reference should be made for the following facts also.

of a community, but it encouraged the leaders to try to find ways of doing so.

The first community of women came into existence in 1845, in London, to be followed at intervals by many others. The early days were naturally full of difficulty, both from within and from without. But Pusey sums up the story of these early days thus: 'The striking characteristic of the history, and that which makes it and so much besides that has been hopeful of late years in the Church of England . . . has been the very absence of design. It was not *planned* by man: it originated in the Providential leadings of God. He began: He carried it on: He gave strength: He will give the increase. It was not the work even of thoughtful persons, judging *a priori* that such institutions would be a blessing to the English Church: *it was not planned, it grew*'.

The basic motive for the establishment of the women's communities was the desire to lead a consecrated life. But this fundamental desire was reinforced by various other factors which made active communities of women to be seen as an advantage both to the women concerned and to the Church as a whole.

Partly due to the influence of Florence Nightingale, and the experiences of the Crimean War, by 1863 various women's communities had been founded and were slowly beginning to be recognized as useful and valuable, although there was still a great deal of prejudice and hostility to be overcome. By this time several men also began to feel that the desire for a consecrated life was as strong for them as for the women. Being in the ministry already, they had plenty of outlet for their energies. They seemed to need some additional reason for founding a community. What brought this about was the need for foreign missionary work.

After some experiments both of living together as priests and of retreats, the first religious community for men was founded in 1866. This was the beginning of the Society of St John the Evangelist, otherwise known in Oxford as the

Cowley Fathers. Its founder, Richard Meux Benson, was a remarkable man: a many-sided person: scholar, parish priest, spiritual director, religious founder, and yet with it all so reserved and unself-assertive that even now his life remains largely unknown and hidden—as he would have wished. He wrote: 'Perhaps it is a token of Keble's saintliness that his life is left hidden with Christ in all the obscurity of the original apostles. We cannot now have a biography of him'. These words apply equally aptly to Benson himself.

The view which animated Benson comes out very clearly in the *Instructions in the Religious Life* which he gave to the society during its early years. The volume called *The Religious Vocation* shows his insight into the aim of the community. He lays great emphasis upon 'sanctification' as the main purpose. 'The purpose of my vow is to bind me to Christ in the fellowship of a holy life.' Benson was convinced that nothing less than the divine vocation of the Society would enable its members to persevere, and to overcome the difficulties by which it was surrounded. 'Our Society was not called by human wisdom . . . we feel that God has gathered us, and there is no occasion to give way (i.e. to pressure from without). . . . God does not speak merely for the moment. When he calls into being a thing He will preserve it.' But he insists that this call to a special mode of life comes *in* the Church (though not *from* it):

Our vocation is subordinated to the general call of Christ in His Church. . . . We must remember that our life as Religious is not something over and above the ordinary Christian life. It is only the ordinary Christian Life developed under such regulations as are rendered necessary for individuals because the Church at large has fallen away from her true spiritual calling of conscious union with Christ.

Benson also insists that the 'Religious' is to be specially

'a man of the moment . . . precisely up to the mark of the times . . . most especially of the present moment and its life. His duties throw him entirely into the interests of the present moment. Eternity is in that moment, and all the energies which are given to eternity are given through that moment.' 'This makes such a man accept the age in which he is living. . . . He does not deplore what is happening round him . . . he sees many things to rejoice in, and others as a summons to immediate action—dealing with actual problems of the present day . . . being, as we should say, "on the spot". In this way the religious community bears witness to the present power and reality of God, at this moment, here and *now where we are*.'[1]

If there was one group of men who understood the emphasis upon the calling of the Church in the world of its own day, it was those Cambridge scholars who succeeded the early Tractarians. B. F. Westcott, later Bishop of Durham, preached a sermon at Harrow School in 1868 on the theme of the disciplined or ascetic life as the most effective type of Christian life. In it he argued that at the crises of Christian history different types of disciplined life have appeared. He named in turn St Anthony, St Benedict, St Francis of Assisi and, finally, St Ignatius Loyola. He did not give these examples as patterns for the present day, but rather as a suggestion that they needed something *new*. He ended his sermon with these memorable words :

Nothing from old times will meet our exigencies. We want a rule which shall answer to the complexity of our own age. We want a discipline which shall combine the sovereignty of soul of Anthony, the social devotion of Benedict, the humble love of Francis, the matchless energy of the Jesuits, with faith that fears no trial, with hope that fears no darkness, with truth that fears no light.[2]

[1] *The Silent Rebellion*, p. 251.   [2] *Ibid.*, p. 222.

The Anglican Communities

This revival of the 'religious' life in the Anglican Church during the nineteenth century was a remarkable phenomenon. As A. M. Allchin says, those who answered this call 'by their religious profession brought into the open that silent rebellion against the tyranny of evil and the conventions of the world, to which every Christian is pledged by his baptism'. These communities, and those which have been born later, are now an integral element in Anglican church life. Some of the earlier communities—often for quite natural reasons—gradually faded out. But many have found new ways of expressing their vocation in the modern world, and are alive and influential at the present time. Since 1945 several new communities have been born and are showing signs of vigorous life. The quality is so great that it is only possible to give a passing mention to one or two examples which suggest the breadth of vision and the depth of spiritual life which lies behind it.[1]

Among the many women's communities, that of St Mary the Virgin, with its Mother House at Wantage in Berkshire, is the largest, having schools, homes for the sick and parochial work in England, India and South Africa. Similar work is done by the large Order of the Holy Paraclete.[2]

The Society of St John the Evangelist (still known popularly as the 'Cowley Fathers')[3] continues to expand. Worldwide in spirit from the very beginning, its interest now includes valuable service to the Ecumenical Movement on its deeper side, particularly through personal contacts, instruction in prayer and the extension of the movement of retreats in Protestant Europe.

[1] A Roman Catholic layman, Mr Peter Anson, provides an excellent survey of these Anglican communities in *The Call of the Cloister* (SPCK).

[2] Order of the Holy Paraclete, St Hilda's Priory, Sneaton Castle, Whitby, Yorks.

[3] The Mission House, Marston Street, Oxford.

The Community of the Resurrection, based on Mirfield in Yorkshire, has gone steadily forward since its inception in 1892, when six priests committed themselves to the new-born community for life. During the first ten years their numbers grew sufficiently for them to begin new work in South Africa, and to found a theological college in England. 'In twenty years the African work included a vast missionary and educational programme in Johannesburg and a growing public school, while the College work had necessitated a University Hostel in Leeds; Rhodesia had been added to the commitments; the fourth and fifth decades (up to 1942) saw the extension of the urban African work in Sophiatown and the locations; and in the last twenty years there have been further additional houses in the Transvaal, Wales and the West Indies.'[1] The community includes brethren from Canada, New Zealand, America, Africa and Bermuda, as well as from the British Isles; and its seventieth birthday (1962) sees a community with seven houses, 87 brethren in the Church Militant, and 44 in the Church beyond.

The work of this community in South Africa has brought it world-wide fame, through the publication in 1956 of Trevor Huddleston's book *Naught for Your Comfort*. 'Never before had a prophet arisen to expose the horrors of the city of gold. A great measure of the effectiveness of this book was due to the fact that it was not the cry of an isolated visionary, but that it emerged at white-heat from the furnace of fifty years solid, unromantic, back-breaking work by a community.'

What is the secret of this vital growth in little more than half a century? The community answers: 'The secret . . . is the call of God to the founder and his sons and brethren to plunge their freedom to own, their freedom to marry, and their freedom to choose, into the ocean of the Love of

[1] Quotations are from *The Moving Waters, 1892-1962* (Mirfield Publications).

God. The energy is the working of the Holy Spirit. There is no other explanation.'

The same 'secret' explains the growth and expansion of other communities like the Society of the Sacred Mission, which has doubled its numbers since 1945, and has launched out into full-scale work in Australia, including a new theological college.[1]

The Society of St Francis has more than doubled its numbers since the end of the war. In addition to increasing activity in this country, it has extended its sphere of service to the mission in New Guinea.[2]

This apostolic expansion of the religious life is coupled with an increasing sense of the sin of disunity. Prayer for unity, resulting in contact with other churches and with people from very different backgrounds, is characteristic of many communities. The Sisters of the Holy Cross at Haywards Heath in Sussex, for instance, is an older community which springs directly out of the Oxford Movement, and had a period of very active mission work at home and all kinds of social service, but it is now a centre of worship on the Benedictine model, with prayer for unity as its main 'concern'. This spirit should indeed be the heart of the religious life, for in the words of Father Benson, it 'should focus the love which ought to animate the whole body of the Church Catholic'.

A significant feature in the development of community life in England is the growth of contemplative communities. Several (such as Burnham Abbey, West Malling, Fairacres near Oxford and others) are women's communities.[3] There is also a small beginning on the men's side at Crawley in Sussex. The importance of this element in our church life,

---

[1] Society of the Sacred Mission, Kelham, near Newark, Notts.

[2] Society of St Francis, Cerne Abbas, near Dorchester, Dorset.

[3] Burnham Abbey has sponsored a multi-racial foundation in Basutoland, with European and African women in one community.

when millions of our fellow-countrymen ignore God entirely, and when anxiety, materialism and evil are rampant, cannot be over-estimated.

Some of these contemplative communities have been in existence for a long time. Others are comparatively new. For instance, in 1914 two women formed a 'Confraternity of the Hidden Life'; in 1918 this small group, slightly larger now, took a small house and lived a life of prayer together. In 1923 this small beginning had developed into a contemplative community which by this time had moved to Tymawr (near Monmouth). By 1932 the Rule and constitution were completed, and the 'society now consists of contemplatives who live in the House and make their profession for life; and of oblates who live under rule, while continuing their work in the world. There are also associates.'

'The Oxford Movement', says Professor Owen Chadwick, 'changed the external face and the internal spirit of English religious life. These changes succeeded in transforming the atmosphere of English worship, in deepening the content of English prayer, in lifting English eyes to the treasures of the Catholic centuries, whether ancient or modern.'[1] The religious communities have played a great part in this transformation. It is evident that in this revolutionary age the Church in England needs them more than ever.

New British Communities

In addition to the development of Religious Orders within the Anglican Communion, some new movements have arisen during the twentieth century. Fundamentally, they have a similar aim, but their expression is very different.

Historically, the *Iona Community* comes first, because the history of the island of Iona off the western coast of Scotland itself represents in miniature the whole course of the religious development which we have been tracing down the

[1] *The Mind of the Oxford Movement* (Black), p. 58.

centuries.[1] Through St Patrick and St Columba Celtic monasticism was the fruit of the religious life of Christian Gaul, which again (through Cassian) goes back to the Desert Fathers. St Columba was an outstanding figure in the Celtic Church—a very prince among men.

There were Columban monks and missionaries in Iona for nearly six hundred years. During the later Middle Ages they were constantly harried or devastated by Viking raiders from Scandinavia. Then came the Roman period when there were Benedictine monks at the Abbey, and the Augustinian Rule at the Nunnery. When the Reformation came to Scotland all the monasteries were suppressed in 1561. So the last monks disappeared, and gradually the monastic buildings fell into ruin.

The restoration of the abbey in Iona began about 1900. Now the rest of the monastic buildings, including the cloisters and the Chapel of St Michael, have been restored by the Iona Community, with the help of gifts from people all over the world.

From time immemorial Iona has been a holy place; it was a centre of pilgrimage, an 'isle of saints' and the burial-place of kings. One looks across white sands and blue-green water to mountain peaks on other islands and on the mainland. On the seaward side one looks out across the Atlantic, knowing that the nearest land is the coast of Labrador. Iona may be small, but its outlook is vast. Fortunately it is not too easy to reach. So in spite of tourist steamers which call for a few hours in the summer, it retains an atmosphere of simplicity, of a 'place apart'. The natural situation is indescribably beautiful. Storms rage round its ancient rocks, and it abides, unshaken. Calm days follow when the air is gentle and the sky serene. (A photograph faces p. 32.)

The modern community came into being in 1938. It arose

[1] See T. R. Morton, *The Iona Community Story* (Lutterworth Press), and George MacLeod, *Only One Way Left* (Iona Commnuity). The address is Iona, by Oban, Argyll, Scotland.

out of a time of great distress in Glasgow and the district. Their leader was the Rev. George MacLeod of Govan. Eight men—four parsons and four laymen—decided to go to Iona as a committed group to rebuild the monastery there. Many people thought they were mad. 'What on earth are these young men after? Are they "going over to Rome"? What does it all mean?' But George MacLeod knew what he was doing, and so did the young men who joined him. On Iona a life of corporate and personal devotion had been lived for a long time, with no artificial distinctions between the sacred and the secular. The ruins of the Roman monastery were a mute reminder of the days of the medieval unity, and called them to find a new unity in the universal Church of our own day. The Reformation period reminded them of their personal vocation, which they now intended to renew in the spirit of their predecessors on that island. 'On Iona a task was waiting to be finished. It was a task that was significant, symbolic and practicable. The object of going there was to learn, in a true community life, how the Church should live and work in the world today.' Those who founded the community desired to help to answer Columba's dying prayer :

Unto this place, small and mean though it be, great homage shall yet be paid, not only by the kings and people of the Scots, but by the rulers of foreign and barbarous nations and their subjects. In great veneration too shall it be held by holy men of other churches.

The Iona community has been described by its own members as 'a modern movement, anchored to the ancient Faith : seeking to preserve the eternal elements in our Reformation principles in danger of being lost', and also 'seeking to re-assert those Catholic (i.e. universal) elements in our Faith that will alone be adequate for that united world which, through the trials of the present time, is even now being brought to birth'. Or, again, 'the Iona Community is a body of men, ministers and craftsmen, who are committed through their life together, and in their own work, to seek the way of obedience to Jesus Christ, whereby the Church may fulfil her mission in the world today. The members of the Iona Community are bound together by the common experience of a life shared in work and worship on Iona, by a common intention in their work on the mainland, and by a common discipline.'[1]

This community is not residential, save in the summer months when as many members as possible live and work there together. For them all, the island is their 'home' as well as the place where they are trained in the life and spirit of the community. The community has a threefold Rule which concerns prayer and Bible reading, the use of time and the use of money. This is not a mere 'time-table', but a determined effort at self-discipline in order to bring the whole of life under obedience to God, and thus to be set free for his service. (A photograph of some worship faces p. 64.)

Membership is open both to ministers and laymen, and also to men belonging to all churches. In practice, however, the majority of the members are in the ministry of the Church. They work in Scotland and in other countries, as well as overseas in missionary and social work and in education. In 1962 there were about 150 full members. Wherever possible the members meet for a day once a month, and go to Iona every summer. Those abroad try to arrange meetings of the same kind in their own region.

As the community life has developed a great many people in many lands have desired to be connected with it. These people are now gathered together under the term 'Associates'. They are men and women, ministers and lay folk, and there is a special youth branch as well. All accept the devotional discipline of the community and commit themselves to a definite participation in the life and work of the community. They make the promise: 'By the power of God

[1] T. R. Morton, *What is the Iona Community?*, p. 3.

and in company with other seekers, I dedicate myself anew to a closer discipline in response to His free gift to me of life'.

As the years have passed the aim has widened. It is concerned with nothing less than *wholeness* : with the whole of life and with the whole Church. In a broadcast talk, Dr N. Micklem said : 'This Iona Movement is all of a piece : the rebuilding of the old ruins, the coupling of intellectual work with manual, the bringing of the common loaves to Church, the fishing-nets round the Holy Table (at another centre), the direct prayer, the insistence that politics and craftsmanship and economics and drama and home religion are not to be separated, the holy indignation that the Church has become to some considerable extent a coterie out of touch with life, a "Sunday affair", a self-contained bit of the national life'. He pointed out that Dr MacLeod insists that 'this social concern does not blunt the personal question, it only serves to sharpen it. . . . In effect the problem of prayer becomes more intense, the understanding of our Bibles becomes more urgent, public worship more essential, and the sacraments more desperately needed for our souls and for the ingrafting of our children.'

Thus the Iona Community is profoundly concerned with the present and its needs and demands. It also looks forward to the future. The symbolic statue in the cloisters at Iona, the *Descent of the Spirit*, is prophetic. In the words of George MacLeod : 'If a new reformation be upon us, how are we to put ourselves in the way of recognising the new descent of the Spirit as it comes? The only way is to get the new answers for our obedience to God at those points where He is really speaking to us. This is how we must move towards our A.D. 2000. Only so can we be put into the way of the Descent of the Spirit for our time.'

St Julian Community is a small women's community which has been established in the south of England for several years.[1] Since 1950 it has been settled in a long, low country house near the village of Coolham, in Sussex. In the seventeenth century this was a farmhouse. Later owners have added to it, very skilfully, so that all the later additions face south, with a wide view over quiet country, to the line of the Downs against the sky. The house stands in large grounds, and has a beautiful garden and a lake of its own, with swans and herons and other waterfowl. The whole place is full of peace. Yet the village is close at hand, with its Norman church and its Quaker meeting house where William Penn used to worship. (A photograph faces p. 33.)

St Julian's grew out of the experience and vision of Florence Allshorn, who had lived as a missionary in Uganda for a short time between the two wars. She was sent to a small isolated village in the heart of a swamp, alone with one other senior missionary. Here she went through a painful and testing experience. Not only was the 'senior' woman difficult to live with, but her violent outbursts of temper frightened the Africans, and made any mission work difficult. It was here that Florence Allshorn learned the one thing which was to govern the rest of her life and thought : 'She realised that a missionary who goes abroad to witness to a God of Love can do no effective work if she cannot learn to love those with whom she lives'. So at once, she made it her practice to read the great chapter on love in the Letter to the Corinthians, constantly, and she prayed that she might learn that love. Gradually, the situation changed; and 'in that ugly swamp she created a really happy home'.

After three years Florence was invalided back to England with T.B. After a prolonged course of rest and treatment she recovered, and was appointed Principal of a CMS training college for women, where she worked, very fruitfully, for twelve years. It was during these years in London

[1] See J. H. Oldham, *Florence Allshorn and the Story of St Julian's*, and *The Notebooks of Florence Allshorn* (SCM Press).

that the idea of St Julian's was born. This was due to the
fact that so many of the young women she had trained came
back after their first spell of work abroad not merely tired,
but disillusioned and disappointed. She longed to be able to
give them a time of healing and quietness, in order that
they might face life again with new courage and joy.

The first house, Oakenrough, stood high up on the hill
above Haslemere; here Florence Alllshorn and her three
friends began the community life. After some years Oakenrough became too small, and the community moved to a
larger house at Barns Green in Sussex. Here the community
began to grow in various directions. Some of the people who
came to rest found that they needed more than this, so
groups were formed—some of which still meet—for study,
prayer and mutual discussion. The guests were usually missionaries, and these days of intellectual, as well as spiritual,
reading and reflection sent them back with a new vision and
a wider outlook to face the difficulties of the post-war period.
Many other people began to come : clergy and ministers,
teachers and lawyers, doctors and church workers, and also
a stream of visitors from other countries—Africans and In-
dians and Chinese and Germans and Americans and Swedes,
till as one of them says : 'The community began to be
known on the continent and in the far corners of the earth
almost better than in England'.

The *work* of St Julian's is the guest house, and all that this
involves of hard work and many personal contacts. The *life*
of the community, from the point of view of its aim, goes
on out of sight. In a lecture Florence Allshorn gave on the
purpose of the community, she said :

Some of us will have to enter upon a vow of dedication to the
Eternal which is as complete and irrevocable as the vow of the
Middle Ages. Little groups of dedicated lives, knowing one
another in fellowship with the divine will, yet not wholly of the
world. Religion has got dulled and cooled and flooded with the

secular. It must be lit and fired and flooded with the Eternal. They must be ready to go the second half, obedient, sensitive, selfless. Such groups will re-create the Christian witness.

With no outward signs of a traditional community, the marks are there all the same. The members of the community have their Rule. Silence is kept in the house after prayers in chapel till after breakfast next morning. It is during this time that the Sisters pray and worship together and in private. Each has a day off once a week, which has to be spent away from the house. Part of the annual holiday is spent in solitude. It is evident that prayer comes first in their ordered life; manual work is necessary both in the house and on the farm. Care is also taken to do some intellectual work. The balance between prayer and worship—the 'work of God'—and intellectual and manual labour is Benedictine in spirit, in a modern setting.

The vow of fidelity to the aim of the community is not the threefold vow of the Religious Orders. In practice, however, the members find they have to be 'celibate'; they aim at simplicity instead of 'poverty', and sharing what they have with those who need it; and they are obedient to the community (very rarely does the warden have to make a final decision). And although this is not laid down as a rule, each member who is accepted after a period of probation regards this as a life vocation. The fact that some members have given up very skilled professions to do this, shows the seriousness with which they regard the vow they have made.

St Julian's is still a small community; but it has already founded a branch house in Kenya. This was started in 1956, when the situation there was very critical: the Mau Mau trouble was coming to an uneasy end, and the Europeans were apprehensive. When they heard that St Julian's was proposing to open a centre where all races could meet, there was violent opposition. For the first eight months the atmosphere was stormy, but all the external difficulties were overcome, the members of the community safely installed, both physically and legally. Since then the house has proved its value in the tense situation. Here Africans, Asians and Europeans meet each other in a friendly atmosphere, and find that friendships can be formed and mutual understanding increased. For instance, a weekend was arranged for a small group of women students: three Africans, three Asians and three Europeans. It was a happy time, in which the members of this group shared in picnic meals, games, discussions and worship. In Nairobi itself one community-member has a centre for multi-racial meetings, which often leads to fresh contacts with Africans and Asians who would not otherwise find their way to Limuru. Missionaries from all societies visit the house a great deal, and are thankful for the rest and refreshment it provides. Here people of many races find something of that peace which is distinctive of the mother house in Sussex.

As St Julian's looks out into the future, its hope is to move into its 'next twenty-one years, without blueprints, alert as Florence Allshorn was to the way that love can still be the motivation and inner impetus of our response to whatever the future holds out to us'.

In a quiet hollow in the cliffs, beyond the weird Valley of Rocks in North Devon, stands a large country house, *Lee Abbey*.[1] The entrance is imposing: a tower and a gateway which appear to lead to some ancient castle or manor house. But the impression is misleading. The house is scarcely a century old, although there used to be a seventeenth-century manor house on the same spot. The land on which it stands was once the property of a Cistercian monastery, Ford Abbey. The view from the present house is extremely beautiful. Sheltered from the fury of winter gales, the house

[1] See Jack Winslow, *The Lee Abbey Story* (Lutterworth Press). The address is Lee Abbey, Lynton, North Devon.

has a background of green and wooded hills. In front the grassy meadows slope steeply down to a little rocky bay walled in by great cliffs, and beyond is the sea, stretching away to the west. (A photograph faces p. 33.)

Thousands of people come here every year. Winter and summer, there is a constant flow of visitors of all kinds. What do they come for? In order to answer this question, we turn to the history of the present community. Outwardly the gay and carefree atmosphere of a holiday house does not seem to suggest a 'religious' community of any kind. But no one can be long there without feeling a very different atmosphere: something quiet and friendly and something more, to which newcomers can scarcely give a name. The fact is that behind all the fun and laughter and freedom is a disciplined, dedicated, hard-working community of men and women. In working and living together in the service of God and the Church, they have found a new way of life.

Lee Abbey grew out of the prayers and dreams of two men who were soon joined by others, and together formed a close-knit team. Their 'concern' was for a real spiritual awakening within their own Church, the Church of England. As they thought and prayed together they began to see that what was needed was a 'spiritual powerhouse', a 'place to which large numbers of men and women would come, and from which they would go forth with new-found faith and life to quicken others in their turn'.

Their dream came true on 6th June, 1946, when the Bishop of Exeter dedicated Lee Abbey to the service of God. It was not a monastery, it is true, but it *was* intended to be a 'religious house', consecrated to the work of God.

From the outset it was evident that a large number of people would be needed to run the house, garden and farm; the practical side was clearly envisaged and organized. Far more important was the quality of the people who would do all this work. The leaders saw that these people ought to be sincere Christians, prepared to live a disciplined Christian

life : people who would see all their work, from the highest
to the lowest kind, as a witness to Christ, for whom the
house exists. Thus gradually the 'Lee Abbey Community'
came into being. At the centre is a group of men and women
who stay for several years, some perhaps as a life vocation.
All who come to work at Lee Abbey are expected to be willing to become part of the community. So from the beginning
they accept a simple Rule of life, even if they cannot stay
very long.

Each member works out his or her own Rule of life under
the guidance of the warden, and the discipline of personal
and corporate life is carefully maintained by corporate worship, regular Bible study, sacramental Communion and the
insistence on honest and loving relations with the rest of
the community. The result is a quality of life which creates
an atmosphere of freedom, friendship and happiness, which
makes a deep impression on all who come to stay at the
abbey.

The missionary and pastoral aim of Lee Abbey is carried
out mainly through Holiday House Parties in the summer,
and in other conferences. Every year more than three thousand people pass through the house. The spirit of Lee Abbey
is ecumenical, and people from varying points of view feel
at home here. One Roman Catholic priest stayed here, and
said he felt more at home at Lee Abbey than in many other
places which were more conventionally 'religious'. 'Miracles'
happen at Lee Abbey. Why? The leaders say : 'We are quite
ordinary people'. But they are 'ordinary people' who work
as a team, in real fellowship, who proclaim Christ in all his
love and power, who base all their teaching on the Bible as
the living word of God, and believe (and act upon it) in the
constant overruling guidance of the Holy Spirit.

This alone explains the fact that after the first ten years of
life Lee Abbey goes on from strength to strength. In the
summer season the house is filled to overflowing. Hundreds
of people who have been to the Abbey have been revitalized,

and have gone back to their homes and work and parishes to bring new life to others. Lee Abbey has indeed become a spiritual power-house, and many of the people who have been revitalized are now also being trained and equipped to do much more effective Christian service than ever before.[1]

[1] Scargill House in Yorkshire, near Skipton, carries on the same life and work in the north of England.

3

New Communities within Continental Protestantism

THE emergence of new religious communities within the Reformed (or Presbyterian) Churches in Switzerland and France is an astonishing phenomenon.

In the main, apart from the fact of decadence in the life of the monks and nuns, and the abuses which had weakened their witness, there were two main theological reasons for the rejection of monasticism at the Reformation. It was felt that the existence of the Religious Orders contradicted the doctrine of 'justification by faith'; and the stern discipline of the monastic Orders was held to be opposed to the liberty of the Gospel, which was for every man, without exception. Further, strong objection was raised against the division of Christian people into two categories: the 'elect', who choose the 'way of perfection', i.e. the religious life, and the 'ordinary' Christian, who lives 'in the world', and has to get on as well as he can on a lower level.

Speaking generally, this rejection of monasticism has been taken for granted in the Reformed Churches of France and Switzerland. Now and then men and women who were seeking a deeper spiritual life formed groups for prayer and Bible study and tried to live under a simple Rule, but these groups usually faded out.

During the nineteenth century one or two thoughtful men realized the gap caused by the rejection of monasticism. Harnack, for instance, although he understood the Reformers' attitude, saw clearly that in any community there is always a need for some persons to devote themselves entirely to its aims :

Thus the Church claims its volunteers who abandon every other calling and dedicate themselves wholly to the service of others, not because they think this is a 'higher' vocation, but simply because it is necessary, and because an impulse of this kind ought to spring from a living Church. But the rigidity of anti-catholic feeling has stifled any such impulse in the Protestant Churches. We have paid too dearly for this. . . .[1]

Kirkegaard has several references to this gap. 'The monastery was allowed to die out, and now we stumble about in the dark, not knowing where we are.' Here is a prophetic passage :

There is no doubt that the present time, and Protestantism always, needs the monastery again; there is no doubt that it should exist. The 'monastery' is an essential dialectical fact in Christianity and we need to have it there like a lighthouse, in order to gauge where we are . . . If there is to be true Christianity, in every generation, there must be individuals to meet that need.[2]

Less than a hundred years later, this prophetic insight was fulfilled in the founding of two religious communities within the Reformed churches : one for men and the other for women. They came into being quite independently; now they are so closely united that in essence they are one. They use daily the same prayer-book, they have the same constitution, and they live by the same Rule. Taizé is in France, and Grandchamp in Switzerland.

The Taizé Community

Taizé is a small remote village in Burgundy. It stands upon a hill, and the village street straggles steeply down to

---

[1] A. Harnack, *Das Wesen des Christentums* (1900 ed.), p. 180.
[2] *Journal* for 1847 and 1848, nos. 1123 and 711.

the valley below. From the highest point of the ridge there
is a spacious and beautiful view over quiet country : vine-
yards, woods, meadows and scattered villages and hamlets.
The landscape reminds one of Somerset and Devon, but the
presence of the vines, and the architecture of the villages and
their churches, are distinctly French. Peaceful as it looks
today this countryside was the scene of much violence and
bloodshed during the Middle Ages. Burgundy was a great
historic dukedom, finally united to France in 1477. Its significance for Europe lies in the realm of the spirit. The ruins
of the great abbey of Cluny are only a few miles from Taizé.
Further away in the opposite direction lies Cîteaux, with its
wealth of memories of St Bernard.

The founder of the modern Taizé community, Frère
Roger Schutz, is of French and Swiss parentage. He is a
'son of the manse' and grew up in a very happy home, 'full
of books and full of charity'. At one time, during his school-
days—when he had no special faith of his own—he boarded
with a Catholic family. While he was with them he received
two impressions which never left him : one was the scandal
of division within the Christian Church, and the other the
sheer goodness of this family and the reality of their Christian faith. Later, he became a convinced Christian. Very
soon he knew that he was called to the ministry. While he
was studying theology at Lausanne—a course of study which
was often interrupted by illness and long periods of conva-
lescence—he read and thought a great deal. The result was
that he became sure that he was called by God to revive the
monastic life in some form. He said to the present writer :
'I was convinced that the *strength* of monasticism was fundamental; that it was a great force, and that the Church could do
great things with bodies of men, united by vows, to a lifelong
fidelity. . . . I was *convinced* of this. So I felt that I must
restore to the Church this element which had been rejected.'

This was not an easy decision to make, for all his religious
and theological training was dead against monasticism. The

Morning service in Iona Abbey

The Ecumenical Sisters of Mary, Darmstadt

La Cittadella, Assisi

Taizé

more he thought about it, the more he saw that monasticism contains two vital principles : (*a*) At its best, the Religious Orders have always been open to the world—to the whole world—to men and women in their actual daily life, in their need and suffering and distress. (*b*) Monasticism is always 'at the heart of the Church'. He knew that a small community must work out these two principles in its own life. As he reflected, he felt the difficulty of founding a community which would keep these two basic principles always in view, for he had nothing to 'go by'—no such community existed within Protestantism, nor had there been any in the 400 years since the Reformation. But he saw that if these two principles were incarnated and united in a religious community the monastic life would never be a flight from the world. Rather, the world would eventually come into the Church. Thus the strength of such a community is to be a centre of unity. Further, the monastic life ensures continuity. 'Movements' arise, do their work, and pass away; but a religious community goes on from one generation to another : as one leader disappears, another comes forth and carries on. The community lives on because 'its life is preserved and carried forward by prayer'.

Seeing his vocation so clearly, in 1940 Frère Roger chose the centre for the new community in the almost derelict village of Taizé, in Burgundy. For a time he lived alone, doing all he could to help refugees to escape from France to safety. In 1942 the Germans occupied the whole of France, and the activities of the Gestapo made his work impossible. So he went back to Switzerland, continued his theological studies, and then in 1944 he returned to Taizé, with one or two recruits for the new community. Five years later, in 1949, the first seven Brothers were 'professed'. In 1952-53 Frère Roger, now the prior, composed the Rule, which expressed the essence of their vocation.

From the outset the Brothers saw that Christian unity was a fundamental element in their work. Already in 1941 the

c

first ecumenical contacts with Roman Catholics had been made, when Abbé Couturier and Père Villain visited Taizé. The local bishop (of Autun) allowed the Brothers to use the Catholic church in their village for their worship. Over the years this ecumenical spirit has increased to such an extent that in the sphere of Christian unity Taizé is 'a city set on a hill'. In 1962 a new chapel was built by young Germans as a sign of their desire for reconciliation. The crypt is used by the Roman Catholic Church, and Orthodox, Anglican and Protestant representatives from many lands attended the consecration ceremonies together with Roman Catholics, including the Bishop of Autun.

Though their numbers are still small (about fifty), Brothers of different nationalities, French, German, Dutch, Swiss, Danish, Belgian and American, have gone out into all the world in answer to calls from churches or movements : to the Ivory Coast and Algeria, as well as to special work in industrial areas of France and in Switzerland, Germany and the United States. There is a small 'fraternity' in England, in Sheffield. Usually those who 'go out' thus are small groups of two or three, living as fraternities among the people to whom they go, and earning their living by the work of their hands. Their life is often very hard. They can only keep it up because they are rooted in faith and prayer and upheld by the threefold commitment : celibacy, community of goods and acceptance of the authority of the prior. They know that the vows are essential. Nothing but total commitment for life will keep the community alive and fresh, enabling it to be of use in the world.

The Brothers who live at Taizé carry out their calling in different ways. One is the doctor for the district; another has brought much help to the villagers by his skilled interest in co-operative farming. (The Brothers have handed their farm over to a co-operative.) Others are professional potters, and their pottery is sold all over France; others are pastors and theologians. Several Brothers are needed for the actual work of the community in Taizé itself, with its large number of contacts with the world outside, through visitors and through correspondence.

During the day the Brothers wear ordinary clothes, but in chapel they wear a white habit. They meet for worship three times a day : at 7 a.m., noon and 7 p.m. The worship is partly liturgical, partly free and partly silent. No one who has been present can forget the sense of freshness and reality, of solemnity and joy, which breathes through every act of worship. Prayer, both corporate and personal, is the heart of the community.[1] (A photograph faces p. 65.)

In addition to the life of the 'fraternities' the Taizé Community has branched out in two other directions. Through their contact with people of all kinds, and their awareness of the perplexities of so many thoughtful people, Christian and non-Christian, they came to see that they ought to provide a meeting-place for people to come together for study, thought and prayer, in freedom, and with plenty of opportunity for quiet talk and relaxation. This concern has materialized in the new settlement or conference centre of Cormatin, a large village about three miles from Taizé. The new building stands on a grassy ridge above the village, with wide views over fields and woods. At the heart of the low modern building there is a small, ancient chapel, a place of quiet for meditation and personal worship.

Already this new centre is taking shape; it is being used for youth groups, for retreats and for conferences. As the prior says : 'The *Rencontres* of Cormatin seek to communicate a broadminded spirit of adventure, a thirst for a clear insight into the social problems of today, as well as to give factual information, devoid of prejudice, and thereby train

[1] The *Taizé Liturgy* has been translated (Faith Press). Books by Frère Max Thurian of Taizé are also available in English : *Confession* (SCM Press), *Marriage and Celibacy* (SCM Press) and *The Eucharistic Memorial*, 2 vols. (Lutterworth Press). The address is Communauté de Taizé, près Mâcon, Saône et Loire, France.

men to tackle these problems with the constructive methods of present-day sociology.' Cormatin has welcomed some ecumenical conferences, both Catholic and Anglican, as well as visitors from many parts of the world. The problem of running the centre on the domestic side is met by a group of local ladies. They are Catholics, but they offer this work as an ecumenical service.

Cormatin is a door opening out on to the whole world. At Taizé itself, from the very beginning, the door has been open to the whole Church. The first contacts with Roman Catholic bishops and priests have gradually developed into real friendship. In September 1960 this quiet movement flowered into an event. For the first time for 400 years— since the Reformation—Catholics and Protestants came together to see how they could meet the deep religious need of their own country, France. Several archbishops and bishops met 65 Protestant pastors for some days in private. Reporters from the great Paris papers flocked to the village. But all they could see were prelates and pastors walking along the village street, evidently on the best of terms. Jean Guitton wrote : 'It is a sign of the times, a sign of hope. The hope of our day is to see Christianity adapting itself to the new needs of a world in transition.'

An event of this kind, leading to further meetings, could only take place because the Brothers of Taizé believe that 'visible unity is not a mere aspiration, but obedience to Christ'.

The Community of Grandchamp

In 1931 a small group of women met at Grandchamp, a little hamlet near the village of Areuse, about fifteen miles from Neuchâtel, for three days of silence, prayer and meditation. They were drawn together by a common purpose : for all of them prayer had already become the most precious and the most important thing in life. They had a great desire for a deeper spiritual life, in order that they might be enabled to give a clearer Christian witness, both in their daily life, and in the service of the Church. This retreat was the first ever held in this branch of the Reformed Church; it was destined to have far-reaching and unforeseen results.

The first sign of a new movement came five years later. In 1936 one of the original retreatants opened a house of prayer in one of the old houses at Grandchamp, and was soon joined by others.[1] It became evident that this small Retreat house, the only one of its kind in this part of Switzerland, met a great need, and pastor Marc du Pasquier, at the celebration of the tenth anniversary of the house of Retreat, spoke of Grandchamp as 'the Upper Room of the Church'—thus recognizing the ministry of prayer as part of the work and life of the Reformed Church in Switzerland. Meanwhile, the new community was growing, and in 1952 it was formally constituted. During that period Grandchamp owed a great deal to its fraternal contacts with several Anglican communities. An ecumenical link was then forged which becomes stronger and more vital every year.

In 1953 the community of Grandchamp adopted the Rule of Taizé, as it was now evident that the aim of the two communities was the same. Essentially they were one, and they resolved to manifest 'their common unity in thought, prayer and action'. In practice this means that Taizé–Grandchamp is a double community.

Grandchamp is a beautiful setting.[2] Five of the eighteenth-century houses belong now to the community. They have the friendliness of places which for more than a century had welcomed people in need of shelter, as an orphanage and a school. These houses have been adapted

[1] By 1944 the work of the house was becoming overwhelming. The Sisters realized that something new was taking shape, and that they needed more direction and support, so they turned to one of the original members of the first group, Madame Micheli (afterwards Soeur Geneviève, who was installed as Mother Superior in 1952).

[2] The address is Communauté de Grandchamp, Areuse/Neuchâtel, Switzerland.

and modernized. There is a refectory with white walls, a long room where the retreatants gather for addresses and Bible study, a library above the small chapel where the Sisters gather for worship five times a day. At the very heart of the life of Grandchamp is the vast chapel, l'Arche, which has retained the simplicity and austerity of a great barn, with its wonderful timbered roof. The only modern touch is the stained glass which fills the gaps between the beams with narrow panels of deep, rich colour : blue and purple and scarlet. Against the wall a plain wooden cross dominates the whole chapel.

Everything in the community buildings is very clean and bare. Here is a blending of austerity and beauty in that simplicity which is the essence of good taste. The houses are surrounded by gardens and orchards. Some tall poplars, distinctive of this part of the country, seem to stand guard over the little settlement. Behind the hamlet, which lies on a level strip of land, rise a little way off, almost abruptly, the dark pine-clad slopes of the Jura mountains. A clear river flows down from the hills, past the hamlet, out into the lake of Neuchâtel. A winding path, shaded by large trees, runs alongside the river, then passes through thick bushes, till it peters out on a bank of shingle on the shore of the lake. This lake has a charm of its own; it is peaceful and remote, with its stretches of wild reeds and its empty shores. Now and then, in clear weather, the peaks of the Bernese Oberland shine and glitter on the horizon.

There is much peace and quiet at Grandchamp, but it is not 'out of the world' in the usual sense of the word. A few families live in the other houses of the hamlet; children play in the courtyard; people go to and fro to their work. But the spirit of the community pervades the whole place. One quiet corner alone is kept quite private : a garden and a meadow behind the house where the novices live. There is nothing formal about this 'enclosure'. It is simply a quiet place, shaded by large trees, where the Sisters can now and then be by themselves for a little while. Yet there is an invisible 'enclosure', for here the Sisters of Grandchamp are living out the same vocation as their Taizé Brothers : to be both 'present to God' in their prayer and worship, and 'present to the world' in their welcome to all who come seeking peace and new life.

Grandchamp is the mother house of the community. Here the novices are trained. To it the Sisters return from distant places for rest, refreshment and renewal, for Grandchamp is the home of a resident community. Further, since the community developed out of a house of retreat, it is natural that its main work here should be the 'ministry of retreat'.

In 1954 a daughter-house (for German-speaking people) was opened in German Switzerland at Gelterkinden, in the Canton of Bâle. The Sonnenhof is a large house, high up on a wooded hillside, with wide views over green hills and quiet valleys. It is not far from the little town below, but up there it is very quiet, and thus eminently suited to be the site of a Retreat House. In the initiation of retreats in Switzerland the community is carrying out its commitment to be 'present to God', and thus to the Church. From this centre it goes out to the world, as a 'sign' of the presence of Christ in the world he loves.

In the early days of this community the Sisters prayed and waited for some clear direction. It was not long in coming. They saw that they were called 'to go out into all the world' in the form of small groups; living out their vocation in the midst of human distress, unrest and perplexity. This led to the development of 'fraternities'—each in answer to a call, and for a special purpose. These are closely related in spirit to the Catholic 'Little Sisters of Jesus', whom we shall meet in the next chapter. Indeed, this development is due to close contact (in North Africa) between Mère Geneviève of Grandchamp and leaders of this new Catholic movement.

Since 1955 some Sisters have been living in Algiers, where there are now two centres. Here they live as a 'sign' of the love of Christ amidst racial tension. Quite simply, they are there to love and to pray, to be a 'sign' of hope, to witness to the love of Christ for the distressed, the 'down-and-out', and for all who are ignored, or despised.

As in all these small fraternities, some Sisters go out to earn a living, in domestic or social work, or in an office, in order to support the whole fraternity. The others live at home, run the house, and are accessible for all the people who come, at any time of day, for any reason. All are welcomed. These two small centres in Algiers are oases of peace in the midst of hatred and violence.

There is another fraternity at Beirut, in Lebanon. The Sisters were asked to come by one of the pastors there, in order to be a sign of the spirit of Christian unity in a place of so many different communions: Orthodox, Eastern Churches, Anglican, Roman Catholic and Protestant from many lands. They earn their living by running an eye dispensary for the Arab population, in itself a valuable service in a land where eye disease is prevalent.

Nearer home, and most impressive because it represents a bold attempt to carry the life of the Church into the heart of the modern industrial world, is the fraternity of St Ouen, on the outskirts of Paris.

How did this fraternity come into existence? A call came to Grandchamp from a small Lutheran congregation in this district for some Sisters to come and live amongst them, and help the pastor in his difficult work. Gradually the Sisters have begun to enter into the life of their neighbours. The contacts come quite naturally through work in the factory or in the houses where they do domestic work, or in the casual encounters in shops or on the street. Little by little confidence has been gained, and in some instances real friendships are being formed.

The relationship with the pastor and the little congregation is of great value on both sides. The Sisters also help in the church work wherever possible, and they find the Sunday services a spring of life after a week in a completely 'de-christianized' atmosphere. They are aware that any public 'evangelization' in a 'de-christianized' district of this kind will be impossible until it can be done on a united scale, and with much prayer; that means, when the Reformed, Lutheran and Catholic bodies in the district can do it together. At the moment the Sisters feel that their attitude is one of 'waiting' and praying and then using any opportunities, however small, which spring out of their personal contacts with the people round them. They believe that as their lives are lived in prayer, even people to whom they cannot speak of Christ receive something of cheer and courage or help through these actual contacts. This fraternity is a 'sign of the love of Christ in the midst of social misery'.

More recently, in Switzerland itself, a fraternity has been opened in Lausanne. It began with some social work and also through contact with the local church. Out of this experience the Sisters discovered so many lonely women that a fraternity seemed the only way to answer this need. Here the Sisters work closely with the pastors and the local church; they meet for prayer every week and do a good deal of pastoral work.

Behind all this work on the plain of everyday life, there is the fraternity in the mountains. High above a beautiful Swiss valley, with snow peaks all round, blue lakes below, among the larches, there is a small stone Hermitage. Here is absolute solitude. One by one the Sisters go up there in turn, to think and to pray, and thus to maintain, without ceasing, that prayer which is the centre of their vocation: the 'work of God'—in adoration and in intercession. Here they follow Jesus into the desert. Here they climb the mountain to be alone with God. For they know that when they were called into this life the Lord called them first of all to be with him, and then that he might send them forth.

Closely connected with Grandchamp in aim and in spirit

is a women's community in Provence. Its foundress, Antoinette Butte, was formerly a lawyer and a social worker. In 1929 she felt called to give up her professional work, and give herself to prayer. She began her new life alone; those early years were spent in learning and in waiting. Then came the moment when she conducted her first retreat. This opened up a wider ministry within the French Reformed Church, and in 1939 the Protestant Church leaders offered her the Château de Pomeyrol for a retreat house. Meanwhile, other women had joined her in a regular life of corporate prayer, both liturgical and free.

In spite of war-time difficulties and German occupation, this quiet work went on, till the Sisters felt constrained to form a regular community, based on the acceptance of the threefold monastic vow. The first Sisters were professed in 1948 and 1949. Prayer is their main vocation, and the Sisters are also greatly in request within the French Reformed Church for 'Schools of Prayer' and retreats in different parts of France. Latterly the link with Grandchamp has become much closer.[1]

Around these communities there has grown up a group of Tertiaries or 'associates' who are closely connected with their aim. They accept the call to 'pray and work that Christ may reign': first of all in their own lives, then in their parishes and then in the whole Church. Unity is in the forefront of their mission.

It is an interesting fact that the Tertiaries of Grandchamp have a special link with Latin America, for one of their members (from Switzerland) helped to establish a house recently opened in Uruguay. This centre is called *Il Centro Emmanuel*. It owes its inception to the inspiration of Grandchamp, and is intended to serve as a centre for retreats and conferences for the Evangelical Churches of South America.

[1] The address is Communauté de Pomeyrol, Saint Etienne, du Grès, Bas du Rhône, France.

It is also linked with the Department on the Laity in the World Council of Churches in Geneva.

The Basis of these Communities

These communities, although their origins were very different, are now deeply united. The heart of the community lies in its Rule, expressed in the threefold vow, maintained and supported by prayer and obedience. Each community is a small cell in the life of the Church Universal, and in the churches of the Reformation in particular.[1]

The Rule 'contains the minimum without which a community cannot build itself up in Christ, and give itself to the service of God'. The aim of the Rule is not to restrict but to liberate. The purpose of the community as a whole is to be entirely at God's disposal, in order to do his will in the world, in whatever way he may appoint. The spirit of this Rule is one of freedom and movement. The Brothers and Sisters are engaged in a common life which is always moving onward and forward, following Christ. That is, it is a life based on prayer, both personal and corporate, and a life in which the individual finds his or her life enriched by being part of a community, and thus set free from individualism. It seeks to remind all its members continually of their special calling : to be always looking up to God in adoration, and depending on him for strength and direction; and then out to the world in as wide and deep a practical sympathy and love as can be expressed in simple human ways.

In founding these communities, every effort has been made to look forward, and not to be tied to the past; but, in the words of the Prior of Taizé : 'We have been forced to admit that we cannot live out our vocation apart from the total acceptance of these three points : community of pos-

[1] F. Biot, O.P., wrote an account in French in 1959, *Communautés Protestantes* (Editions Fleurus, Paris).

sessions, the acceptance of an authority, and celibacy'. He says that they prefer the word *engagement* (commitment) to 'vow', 'because this word expresses better the essential truth of their personal surrender to Christ, in its totality, by a dynamic movement which is always pressing forward'.

In his book *Vivre l'Aujourd'hui de Dieu*,[1] the Prior of Taizé explains very clearly what this threefold commitment means to the members of both parts of the Community.

Celibacy. This is not so much a refusal of marriage, as a renunciation, in order to live on a 'higher' plane. It is accepted by the members of the community as involved in their call to this kind of life. It is a matter of vocation. The discipline which this involves can only be accepted for the sake of Christ and the Gospel. 'It is only as we keep our eyes fixed on Christ that we can undergo a slow transformation' into a life of love to God and man.

Community of Possessions. 'The bold effort to pool all we possess without being afraid of poverty in the future, and therefore without building up a reserve, gives us an immense strength. But if we begin to save up against the risks of the future, we run the risk of overstraining the Brothers whose vocation it is to live in the present.' Again and again it is clear that 'poverty' is seen as something positive like the Franciscan idea of 'freedom'; its aim is that the community may serve Christ in the world without anxiety, and with a deep sense of dependence upon the Father in Heaven, from whom comes our daily bread, and with that all we need for body and soul. 'For everything which belongs to the Lord is for the use of all.'

Acceptance of an Authority. Obedience is perhaps the most difficult point of all for most modern people. We can see the necessity for it in ordinary human organizations; but the principle of Obedience to a 'Superior' does not come easily to people brought up in a Protestant atmosphere. Yet

[1] English translation: *This Day Belongs to God* (Faith Press).

it is essential for the life of the community. To learn obedience is a way towards maturity; the spirit in which obedience is regarded at Taizé and Grandchamp does not cramp or injure the personality of any one. The authority of the Prior or the Mother ensures both the unity and the continuity of the life of the community; it enables it to be what it is meant to be and to do. All the members of this twofold community agree that these three principles, gathered up in the Rule, are the pivot on which their life depends. They are absolutely essential. Just as marriage vows are taken 'till death us do part', so the *engagement* (commitment) at profession is irrevocable. It is for life.

Above all the Brothers of Taizé and the Sisters of Grandchamp are deeply convinced that 'being' comes before 'doing'. For what is their vocation, ultimately, but the life of love? So they know that everything depends upon each one living 'by, and for God alone'. Thomas Merton puts this very plainly when he says: 'In the night of our technological barbarism, monks must be like trees which exist silently in the dark, and by their vital presence purify the air'. The real life of this community is out of sight. This is suggested by the Prior of Taizé, at the end of his book, when he says: 'Christ alone can kindle in us the fire of his love'. This is the love that moves men to pray and work for Christian unity. This is the love which sends them out into the world, to love and to serve to the utmost. For they never forget that 'at the end of life we shall be judged on nothing but love'.

Lutheran Communities

Now we turn to the Lutheran countries: Scandinavia and Germany. The foundations of the Church in Scandinavia were laid in the dark days of the ninth century A.D. At this time the Vikings were the dreaded pirates and raiders whose name struck terror into the hearts of many lands in Western Europe. Very often they singled out the monasteries for attack, for here were treasures which they coveted. In whirl-wind raids they would often descend upon an undefended monastery, murder the monks, and make off with a great deal of treasure from the shrines of the saints.

In some places men were on the alert, and put up a stiff resistance. But the best resistance of all came from the Church, for here were men who insisted that the best re-sistance would be to turn these 'handsome flesh-eating animals' into Christians. Foremost among these daring men was St Anskar (801-65), a French monk, whose name means 'God's Javelin'. He was one of the most intrepid mission-aries of those early days, for he plunged headlong into the heart of heathen territory. Often repulsed, he kept on re-turning to the attack. When he was made Bishop of Ham-burg he made that city his mission headquarters : from this centre, he 'threw the seeds of Christianity far into Denmark and Sweden'.[1] At the time the results were disappointing, for the 'converts' often had a habit of getting baptized over and over again—apparently as a pleasant change! Needless to say, after Anskar died much of Scandinavia relapsed into heathenism. But his work was not in vain. Indeed it was im-portant, for it prepared the way for the evangelization of Scandinavia about the year 1000. Anskar is often described as the 'Apostle of the North', and he deserves the title. No-where is his memory more firmly cherished than in Den-mark.

At the time of the Reformation (1536) the Church in Den-mark became Protestant and Lutheran. It kept a close link with the earlier tradition, and the change-over was accom-plished quite smoothly. The Church in Denmark has always been proud of its long tradition, going back to the ninth century. But in the twenties of this century some of its mem-bers began to feel a great desire to revive the full heritage of its church life and make it fruitful once more. Out of this 'concern' several 'fellowships' and 'brotherhoods' arose,

[1] H. Daniel-Rops, *The Church in the Dark Ages*, p. 448.

which tried to deepen the reality of faith and worship within their Church.

In 1926 a young theological student went to England, and stayed for a time at Kelham, in an Anglican men's community. His stay there made a deep impression upon him, and when he returned he founded a society called the *Teologisk Oratorium*. This society—which is confined to pastors and theological students—aims at mutual assistance in their own religious life, in order that they may be good priests and pastors. They publish theological and devotional books and articles, and have encouraged the formation of new liturgical forms for public worship.

Soon after the founding of this society in 1932, another similar group was started, to include laymen and pastors who were not already members of the *Oratorium*. This was called the *Fraternitas Sancti Ansgari* (Brotherhood of St Anskar). His name was chosen in order to emphasize the continuity of the Christian tradition in the Danish Church, and also to suggest that these new movements were not seeking to introduce 'novelties' but only to restore and revive the richness of their ancient heritage. As one of them says : 'We wanted to learn from history, and then to bring what we had learned to the present generation, in a form which they could grasp'.[1]

The most important practical result of this new movement has been the establishment of retreats and 'quiet days' in the life of the Danish Church. It also aims at the renewal of the inner life of the Church as a whole, through prayer and the revival of the practice of confession. Other similar movements are being formed; some think that the next step may be the founding of a Lutheran monastery.

Meanwhile, women in Sweden and Denmark had been deeply concerned about the need for a new life in the Church, and especially for greater reality in the practice of

[1] L. Präger, *Frei für Gott und die Menschen* (Quell Verlag, Stuttgart), pp. 196 ff.

prayer. Out of this has grown the Congregation of the
Daughters of Mary.

A woman named Gunvor Norrman was painfully aware
of the dissatisfaction and loneliness of many restless and unhappy women in Sweden. She knew that there was only one
way in which the situation could be met, and that was by
letting them see that such misery is always associated with
self-seeking, and that what these single women needed more
than anything else was to enter into the glorious liberty of
the children of God. At the end of the war she went to Germany, where she found the same situation to an acute degree. The result was that after a time she gathered a group
of some fifteen to twenty women who set to work to try to
live as a community in daily life, in a spirit of peace and
love. Gradually this little society grew, as one after another
came, answering the call of God, giving up good positions
in order to live only for him and his Church. They had
come to the conclusion that 'some people must live wholly
for Christ and the coming of his Kingdom, in order that
other women may come and share in this life of reconciling
love. Only so will they find a new meaning in life, and will
be able to carry the warmth of this love to a cold and hectic
world.'

So out of these years of experiment and probation came
the conviction that they were called to lead a monastic life
'in the world', in the spirit of the three traditional vows or
'Evangelical Counsels', seeking to express them in modern
terms. In 1954 this society was founded. In 1957 it came out
into the open as a community dedicated to a life of prayer.
The mother house, *Nordisk Sambo,* is at Kollund, on the
Danish-German border. They have other houses both in
Sweden and in Denmark. There is also a retreat house open
to women of all kinds who wish to come for quiet and
prayer. As time goes on their life becomes deeper and
quieter; it is a centre for contemplation.

Moving to Germany, let us meet *the Ecumenical Sister-hood of Mary*.[1] (A photograph faces p. 64.)

From the outset this community has been a venture of faith. By faith, under the Hitler regime, the two future Mothers gave up their professional work, in order to be free to do whatever special task God might send them. When this came in the shape of a Bible class for older schoolgirls the outlook did not look very promising. At that moment to do anything of this kind was dangerous; but it seemed the right thing to do and they did it. In spite of the increasing pressure of the political situation and the outbreak of war, they persevered. The small class of six girls grew into a large body of 150, meeting in small separate sections throughout the week; in this way they did not attract attention, which would inevitably have stopped this work alto-gether.

During these years the two friends, Dr Klara Schlink and Frl. Erika Madauss, were learning to walk in the way of naked faith. Often it seemed to them that nothing but blankness lay ahead; they had to go forward from week to week 'not knowing whither they went'. This Bible study was very encouraging, but still they felt something was missing.

Then came the terrible night of the 11-12th September, 1944, when Darmstadt was laid flat in half an hour, and the whole city became a furnace of flame. The next day, stunned by shock and horror, the two friends picked their way amid the smouldering ruins in search of the members of their flock. To their relief they discovered, after a day or two, that most of them were safe. That was all that they could think of for the moment. But when the groups were re-formed the two leaders found that during that night of death, 'something had happened' to these girls. When they could begin to talk about it, girl after girl confessed that she

[1] Oekumenische Marienschwesternschaft, Landstrasse 107, Darm-stadt-Eberstadt, Germany.

had seen her sins as never before. The two leaders told them that they too had felt this, not only in the form of their own personal sins, but the sin of indifference to what had been happening all round them. They felt that they were involved —though they belonged to the Resistance movement in the Church—in the national guilt of the cruelty of the Nazi treatment of the Jews and of many other innocent and helpless people. 'Sins of omission' they now saw in their true light. So this 'godly sorrow' led to a spirit of real repentance in the whole group, and the girls themselves showed its reality in simple practical ways: they began to think of other people, and tried to help the homeless and suffering folk in their own neighbourhood, in a way they would not have done before. Life was coming out of death.

All through that winter of 1944-45, a 'quiet revival' was going on. 'By faith' the two leaders planned a retreat in the forest, about fifty miles away, and the girls agreed to come. It was May 1945: everything was falling to pieces round them, yet they went to the railway station as calmly as if they were simply going off for an outing. They were seeking 'the desert'—quietness and solitude—but the moment they got out of the train they found 'hell let loose': disbanded soldiers, Nazi fugitives and their families, were running for their lives; for their peaceful retreat was close to the battle-front, and the American armies were daily drawing nearer. Overhead and all round them was noise and excitement. But they were not upset. For three days they met for prayer and prolonged meditation, especially on the meaning of the Passion Story. They were kept in peace; it was as though the cloud of God's presence enveloped them.

It was out of this retreat that finally the movement which led to the founding of the community was born. Seven girls —now grown up—said one day, 'Can't we stay together for good?' None of them had thought of such an idea before. Leaders and pupils alike were good Lutherans, with strong Evangelical views; the very idea of the 'religious life' was foreign to them. What should they do? At that moment a Methodist pastor in their neighbourhood became their friend and adviser. He encouraged them to go forward, and told them something about the Brethren of the Common Life at the time of Thomas à Kempis. At this stage he helped them greatly; he died two years later.

Finally, the way became clear to them, and on 30th March, 1947, the small community—seven young women and two leaders—was constituted, with *prayer* as their main work, and *unity* as their message to the Church. So 'by faith', without money or support, they went forward.

They prayed together about everything, and all that was needed came, often in quite unexpected ways. The father of one of the girls gave them a large piece of land for a site, on the outskirts of Darmstadt, on the main road to Heidelberg. The ground was very suitable, flat, on the edge of a forest, with the hills of the Odenwald a few miles away on the horizon. Then they had to build: somehow they were allowed to use rubble for building materials and with the help of many gifts of all kinds the Sisters built their own chapel and their own mother house with their own hands. 'Miracles' happened day after day, but they had many times of hard testing as well. Through all this time of exhausting labour their own community life was being forged into something that would last. And so the community grew, in numbers, in order and in love.

Today they have imposing buildings: among them a fine retreat house for people from all churches, and a large hall— the *Jesu Ruf Kapelle*—in which they perform their religious plays. They had to build this hall because people come in their hundreds, often in special buses, from all over Germany to see them. These plays are wonderful, original, modern in style, moving and impressive, full of the spirit of worship. Other houses are being planned; they want to have a St Francis house as a place of healing for body and mind, for people in great suffering or infirmity. They want to build a reception centre for the hundreds of people who come on Sundays to see the plays, and they would like to have a house for the members of the Third Order, who help the community in many ways.

The Sisters run a printing press for their own publications, which means an immense amount of work. Two sisters are sculptors; they make crucifixes and other figures for church decoration. Others go out two or three times a week to new housing estates where they teach the children, visit the homes, and help people in all kinds of simple practical ways. They also have a house in Israel where they look after old and ailing Jews, for they care deeply for Israel.

All this external activity springs from the heart of their life: *prayer*, both corporate and personal. In addition to the various offices and periods of united intercession, which take up much of their time, each Sister has an hour a day for her own private prayer. The mother house is 'enclosed'; there silence reigns as far as possible for the greater part of the day; there too is a small private chapel, in which they take turns at watching in prayer, while the other sisters are busy outside.

To become a Sister involves a very long period of probation—several years. The Sisters do not take the 'monastic vows' in the usual way, but on the day of her dedication (or 'profession') a Sister wears a bridal wreath and is dressed in white. She then makes a solemn vow of life-long dedication. The Sisters keep their white dresses and wear them on great festivals; otherwise they are simply dressed in grey for work, and black for better use, with little white caps rather like those worn by deaconesses.

The title of the community is significant: the allusion to 'Mary' means that they desire to follow in her steps, in love and obedience, making her prayer their own: 'Behold, the handmaid of the Lord, be it unto me according to thy word'. But why 'ecumenical'? From the very beginning, partly due to the influence of their adviser, Pastor Riedinger, they felt the call to pray and work for Christian unity. This unity, of course, begins at home in their own life as a community; then their hearts go out to all other communities in every communion, and then to the Church as a whole. They are deeply concerned about the sin of disunity, and prayer for unity is a large part of their ministry of intercession. In addition, their retreat house is so arranged that every room speaks of the communion of Saints, or is dedicated to some church by name. For instance, a Benedictine Father may find himself in a room dedicated to the memory of Bonhoeffer, or a Protestant visitor may find herself in a room dedicated to St Catherine of Siena or St Teresa of Avila.

Sometimes people come to this house full of prejudices against this or that body of Christians. The influence of the house and its life of prayer does a great deal—unconsciously —to dispel these feelings, and opens the way for a closer approach to the spirit of unity and love.[1]

[1] Two books by B. Schlink, *The Darmstadt Community* and *Israel My Chosen People*, were published in English in 1963 (Faith Press).

4

New Roman Catholic Movements

'THE Catholic Church continually flowers into a new springtime; she is a notable "sign" to the nations, and from her there streams out an all-embracing light and a gentle love towards all peoples.' These words of Pope John XXIII are not an exaggeration. In this revolutionary age, for the past century and more, new movements have been continually springing up, creating fresh forms of life which minister to the needs of the contemporary world. It is a striking fact that this vitality reaches its peak in Catholic France.

As we have already seen, the French Revolution was a turning-point in the history of Europe. It was the end of one age and the beginning of another. How did the Church fare in this new age? And what of the Religious Orders?[1] As we saw in an earlier chapter, the Orders had frequently been attacked during the eighteenth century; already anti-clericalism was growing. The most notorious instance of this hostility was the act of a 'Catholic Sovereign' (Joseph II of Austria) in the suppression of the Jesuit Order in 1773. He followed this up by closing some 600 monasteries in his realm. The Revolution and the Napoleonic Wars carried the destruction still further.

---

[1] The standard survey is Adrien Dansette, *Religious History of Modern France*, 2 vols. (Nelson). See also A. R. Vidler, *Prophecy and Papacy* (SCM Press).

At the beginning of the nineteenth century, in France and in several adjoining countries, a number of religious houses were still standing, but they were empty and falling into decay. So far as the 'religious life' was concerned, in the dark days of the Revolution it might have seemed to have been extinguished. But it was soon evident that this was not the case: even during the Revolution itself a faithful remnant had not only kept the faith alive, but had begun to plan for the future. When the empire of Napoleon fell, there was a kind of sudden explosion. A revival movement began and continued on an unprecedented scale; the ancient Orders rose like the phoenix from the ashes. New movements were formed: very soon in France alone there were 30,000 monks and 128,000 nuns.

Three of the great Religious Orders were restored. In 1814 the Jesuits (who had been in hiding, some of them as far away as Russia) were allowed to start their life once more in France, and in other countries as well. In 1814 they numbered about 800; by 1820 there were 2,000: by 1850, more than 6,000. This was not merely a growth in numbers: the quality of their life and of their work in education gave them a great influence.

The Order of St Benedict had never entirely faded out; many ancient abbeys still existed; but the Order needed the purifying flame of renewal to bring it once more to life and maturity. The man who led this revival was Dom Guéranger (1806-75), a remarkable man, who had always longed for the monastic life, especially in its Benedictine form. With three friends he settled at the ancient priory of Solesmes. By 1837 Rome gave its approval, and the Benedictine Order was reconstituted in France. Some years later the great sanctuary of Monte Cassino (in Italy) was restored, and once more, new life flowed through the Benedictine Order.

Meanwhile a friend of Dom Guéranger, Lacordaire, who was spending some time in retreat at Solesmes, became convinced that the Dominican Order ought to be revived. This took place quietly in 1839, but by 1870 there were nearly 300 Dominican Fathers.

Although these three restorations are the most celebrated, there were many others. Very few of the congregations which had been active before the Revolution failed to rise again. In a memorable sermon, Lacordaire claimed that 'oak trees and monks are immortal'.

However, there were many difficulties facing the nineteenth-century French Church. Modern French history is one of constant change, intensified by the tragedies of at least three wars upon her own soil. It is as though the waves of the Revolution were still agitating the political and social atmosphere, making it almost impossible for the nation to 'settle down'.

Throughout the latter part of the nineteenth century, the antagonism between Church and State in France stands out as a fact of great significance. It came to a climax with the Act of Separation (9th December, 1905). The enemies of the Church thought that this Act would cause a terrible crisis in the Church. A socialist leader indeed said that it would mean 'virtually the death of the old religion'. Great was the surprise of the anti-clericals when they found that the shock had had the opposite effect. At the time, of course, to many good Catholics it seemed to be a disaster, but later on they saw that it had worked out for the good of the Church in France. In any case, with this Act of Separation the Church moved out into a new era. Gradually the violence of anti-clericalism died down. The Christian Trade Union Movement flourished, and a new youth movement was formed. During the war of 1914-18, the admirable behaviour of so many priests and monks on active service helped to improve relations with the opponents of religion. In 1924, it is true, there was for a time a resurgence of anti-clericalism which was again directed against the Religious Orders, but in the end matters were rearranged to the satisfaction of all concerned, and anti-clerical feeling again died down.

In this improved state of affairs the 'Left' movement in the Church was able to make progress. The Archbishop of Paris, Cardinal Verdier, and the 'red cardinal', Liénart of Lille, did a great deal for the 'red belt'. Both men were greatly respected outside the Church. Throughout this period many members of the Religious Orders gradually came back to France, and their presence and work were tolerated. A Jesuit Father actually stated in 1928 that the laws against the Religious Orders were being 'universally and flagrantly violated'. In 1935, when Laval, the Foreign Minister, went to Rome to sign the Franco-Italian agreement he had an audience with the Pope. This was the first time for seventy years that such a meeting had taken place. Immediately before the outbreak of war in 1939, Cardinal Verdier stated that the 'relations between the Catholic Church and the French State, except for the still unsolved question of education, had never been better'.

France a Mission Field

But even now the Church's difficulties were not over. After the first World War another problem came to the fore. It dates from the industrial revolution of the previous century. Other causes also led to a crisis. The influence of the Russian Revolution of 1917, the widespread economic crisis of 1929, the rising nationalism in countries outside Europe, coupled with the growing awareness of social injustice and all the evils which this involved, culminated in a 'crisis of civilization' in which the Church—in the broadest sense—was involved. The leaders in the Roman Catholic Church were deeply concerned about this situation, for they saw how closely the Church itself was interwoven with the bourgeois Western social structure.

In some countries the Roman Church realized that 'Catholicism had lost its catholicity'. Not only in France, but in all the countries which were at the same stage of economic and social development, the one thing that was evident was the growth of alienation from the Church, and from the Christian faith as a whole. One French priest calls it 'the apostasy of the modern age'.

In France, in the heart of the Catholic Church, the difficulties caused by this 'de-christianization' brought it to a crisis; its leaders were forced to face the situation. This led to a process of renewal. Speaking broadly, this 'renewal' has been furthered by two great waves of apostolic activity. The first, which began in the twenties, led to the rise of 'Catholic Action'. The second, a wave of missionary movements within France, began during the war, and was aided by the Liturgical Movement, and the other spiritual, theological and biblical movements which appeared at the same time.

It is significant that this problem was fully realized and faced while France was at war, and under foreign occupation. In 1943 Christian France had been startled and horrified by the disclosures in a book called *France: Pays de Mission?*.[1] Its authors—two young priests, Godin and Daniel—declared that at least a fourth of the population of France was atheist and that the entire working class suffered from almost complete lack of religion. They maintained that of the adult population of the country only a tenth were practising Roman Catholics.

The Church in France rose to the situation, under the forceful leadership of Cardinal Suhard, whose name will always be associated with this revival of Catholicism in France. In his words and in his writings he urged people to think and to act swiftly : 'The Church today asks of us two things : to *think largely* and to *think quickly*. By "largely" I mean, on a universal scale. Don't be content to follow the example of others : *lead!* . . . We have started a movement and we don't know where it will take us. Get to work!

---

[1] I.e. 'Is France a mission field?' Translated as *France Pagan?* (Sheed and Ward).

Don't stand idle in the midst of the ruins!' (This was in the midst of the war.)

One of the causes and symptoms of de-christianization in France was the lack of clergy. So one of the first moves towards renewal was to awaken and direct a missionary spirit among young priests and theological students. This naturally led to a great emphasis upon the life of the *parish* as the primary cell in the life of the Church. Under the influence of Cardinal Suhard and others the Church set to work to revive a form of ministry which was not altogether new, but had fallen into disuse: the formation of groups of clergy in various dioceses who would live together under a common rule, not as monks but as dedicated men, sustaining and inspiring each other, by praying, studying and working together for the welfare of a large district. Behind this movement was the conviction that it was not possible to have a vital parochial life unless, at its heart, there was a live body of priests. During the years before the war (especially between 1932 and 1933) this idea was being worked out with very good results. For various reasons this movement declined, but it was not dead, and when this new era began men were ready for it.

Some of these renewed societies had a long history behind them. For instance, the remarkable movement, *the Priests of Prado*, was founded in the nineteenth century by an outstanding man, Père Chévrier (1826-79). In 1856, on Christmas Day, he had a sudden 'illumination', which moved him, as he says, 'to follow the Lord Jesus Christ more closely, in order to be able to work more fruitfully for the salvation of souls'. In 1860 he founded a group of priests in a suburb of Lyons, who were to be as closely united as though they were in a community, but who would not take the monastic vows. They were to work entirely amongst the poorest and most unhappy people in their own city. At the heart of this group was a great depth of prayer and dependence on the Holy Spirit. The life of this society grew slowly. Around

1940 it came into its own. Many young and ardent priests have joined it; they all work in de-christianized towns and districts, and in close contact with one another.

Simply to enumerate the various groups or societies of priests who work along these lines would not convey the freshness and vitality which makes them distinctive. Each 'society' has its own particular vocation, its own *ethos*, but the fundamental aim is the same : to be 'priests' in the deepest sense, utterly dedicated to God and committed irrevocably to their calling : to make Christ known in the most neglected and 'godless' parts of the population—in other words, to serve God and man where the need is greatest.

The spirit of these 'priest-missionary' societies may be illustrated from the life of another strong congregation : that of the *Fils de la Charité*. The founder of this movement was Père Anizan (1853-1928). He was ahead of his time, and already perceived that such dedicated priests would be needed in the regions which even then were rapidly becoming de-christianized. He had prophetic insight. 'We have been called into being', he used to say, 'for our own day, and even for the future.' This congregation has a twofold character. All the members are priests, but they also take the monastic vows, and as far as possible lead a common life. Their aim is apostolic. How difficult is their task may be inferred from the following remarks in a letter from a French layman—an ardent Christian—when he heard that one of these priests had been asked to conduct a retreat for priests : 'It's quite daft to prepare a retreat for priests . . . The *curés* are stuffed shirts . . . I can't be bothered with high-sounding theories. It all seems to me very simple : love is simple, and the further we go the simpler it gets. All we have to do is to give everything and to love much. I know I'm very primitive, but I am terribly strong in the love of God.'

From the record of this retreat we catch a glimpse of the kind of world in which these particular priests live and work. They are profoundly aware of the deep gulf which separates the clergy as a whole from the general mass of the population, especially in industrial regions. Some of them have worked for a time, incognito, in factories or at the docks, and they know at first hand what these people really think about the *curés*. Sometimes a scornful remark about a certain *curé* shows this very clearly : 'What would be left of him if he got rid of his cassock!'

All the prejudices against the Church and against the clergy have to be lived down by these 'Sons of Charity' before they can get anywhere at all. So these Brothers try to live and love in a simple human way, sharing the life and interests of the people among whom they live. To carry out their vocation they lay great stress on the importance of their community life. Behind their active pastoral and evangelistic work lies a strict discipline. They examine their life as a 'team', to see if they can discover its weak points. Have they given enough attention to their spiritual training? Does the life of the team go deep enough in personal relationships? Is there anything blocking their fellowship with one another, and therefore hindering their ministry? What are the central convictions which govern their life? How should they be renewed? Behind and above everything else is their life of prayer, both corporate and personal, for themselves and for the world in which they live. Sometimes they ask themselves : 'Have we perhaps failed our people because we have neither taught them to pray as we should nor lived out our own prayer properly?'

It was the growth of such movements which led, in 1941, to the formation of the *Mission de France*. In order to prepare men for the ministry in de-christianized districts the Assembly of Cardinals and Archbishops opened an inter-diocesan seminary at Lisieux—later transferred to Limoges, and then later again to Pontigny (Yonne). By 1954 nearly 400 priests had passed through this seminary, and were already at work in de-christianized regions, both in town and country.

This was the beginning of a wave of missionary movements. Typical of a great many are the kindred movements of the *Frères Missionaires des Campagnes* (Missionary Brothers of the Countryside), founded in 1943 by Father Epagneul, a Dominican, and the *Soeurs des Campagnes*, founded in 1947 for the apostolate of the rural areas.

The work of these Sisters, who are 'Religious' in the full sense of the word, is a sign of a new way of life. In addition to their training as nuns, they all receive a practical training in either domestic and agricultural or similar work. They live in rural centres, in small convents, and earn their living in the ordinary way by going out to work: in the fields, or in the farms, or in the houses of well-to-do farmers. At first the country people did not know what to make of them, but they have now accepted them as 'workers', and friendship and understanding is springing up. In one little country town recently a Sister was elected a town councillor. In order to maintain their life of prayer they have to rise very early, and to return to prayer again in the evening after work. In the winter, when work out of doors is impossible, they have more time for thought and study and they make good use of it. Their life is well balanced.

The 'priest-worker' movement belongs to this period: a movement which began with great enthusiasm, and was later suppressed. One of the most illuminating books on this subject is by Père Loew, who had worked as a docker at Marseilles for some time before the 'priest-worker' movement began.[1] In his diary we get a picture of the close human contact which this one man was able to establish with people living in misery on the fringe of this great seaport. In his view one of the reasons for the failure of the 'priest-worker' movement was the absence of the laity; he is convinced that laymen should take a prominent part in work of this kind. When this movement was banned, Père Loew accepted the restriction, but with great sorrow of

[1] *Journal d'une Mission Ouvrière: 1941-1960.*

heart. He admits, however, that several of the young priest-workers were not properly prepared for the shock of close contact with Communists. Their interest in Marxism often made them neglect their priestly vocation : they 'went too far'.

Later, when the excitement had died down, Père Loew began again. He organized a movement in the south of France, called the 'Industrial Mission of St Peter and St Paul'. Through this mission Père Loew is carrying out his vocation in a new way. Looking back, he can see where mistakes were made, but he believes that this 'cruel set-back' will do the Mission good in the end. For those who are called to this particular life now see that they need to be very practical and level-headed, and above all they see the permanent need for a life of obedience and prayer.[1]

The Story of Charles de Foucauld

Throughout the history of the Church, at every critical epoch, one great figure after another has emerged who is the man for the hour. Whatever the general state of the world at the time may be, he is the leader into a new way of life for the followers of Christ. He recalls them to the centre.

The outstanding figure for the modern age is Charles de Foucauld—precisely because his life and ideals cut clean across the spirit of the age. Instead of noise and hectic activity he sought silence; instead of notoriety and 'success' he sought to be hidden and unobserved. Instead of riches he chose poverty; instead of striving after 'importance' he chose the society of the poorest and simplest people, wanting only to be the 'brother of all'. Above all, instead of looking for 'recognition' or praise or appreciation from men, he sought only to please God. From the moment when he turned entirely to God, his whole desire, through many

[1] See *The Worker-Priests: A Collective Documentation* (Routledge and Kegan Paul) and *Priests and Workers: An Anglo-French Discussion* (SCM Press).

difficult years, was to find out, and follow, and perfectly obey, the will of God. So he lived largely unknown, and when he died it seemed as though there was nothing to show for a life-time of single-minded devotion.

Charles de Foucauld was born in France, in 1858, into an aristocratic family. When he was 5 years old, both his parents died. He and his little sister were sent to live with their grandfather; he was kind and indulgent, but too old to know how to deal with such young children. Charles was a quiet, rather unhappy little boy. In his youth, both at school and at St Cyr (a military academy), and later in the Army, he was very lazy and self-indulgent; he became very fat. As a young officer he was extravagant and wasteful, restless and given to wild pranks. Finally, after a short spell of military duty in North Africa, he became so insubordinate that he had to leave the Army: this was a great blow to his pride as a young viscount and a disgrace for his family. Yet he was very intelligent, and could work when he chose.

After a few weeks of depression, he began to think of the future. North Africa and the desert had already laid its spell upon him. He decided to explore Morocco alone, disguised as a Russian Jew. This project required a great deal of study and expert knowledge; he worked with a will, made the hazardous journey, returned safely to France, and wrote a book upon his experiences which won a gold medal at the Geographical Society in Paris. He was now a 'success'. People wanted to see him and to make much of him. But he remained in seclusion in his Paris flat: all he felt was a great emptiness.

He began to visit churches and to pray: 'O God, if You are the Living God, have mercy upon me. Teach me to know you'. While he was in this state he met a remarkable man, a priest named the Abbé Huvelin; through him, on 30th October, 1886, very simply, Charles de Foucauld, after twelve years of complete unbelief, came back to God. His painful wanderings were over. He had come home.

From that moment, Charles de Foucauld was a different person. He said later : 'The moment that I believed there was a God, I knew I could do nothing else than live for Him wholly; my religious vocation dates from the same moment as the gift of faith. God is so great. . . . To *choose* a vocation is a great misnomer : we do not choose our vocation; we *receive* it.' So Charles surrendered completely : his pride and his self-will were turned into humility and obedience. From this moment his one desire was 'to imitate Jesus'.

The fact of his vocation was quite clear, but it took a long time—several years—for him to learn how to work it out in his life. Knowing that he had a contemplative vocation he tried it out at La Trappe, in a community, and then at Nazareth, as a hermit. He learned a great deal from these experiences, and was grateful for all the care and kindness he had received from so many fine people, but he was still unsatisfied. Gradually the call of the desert, which he had felt so powerfully during his adventure in Morocco, came back to him with increased force. So he went back to North Africa, moved about for a time in the Sahara, and then settled down in a remote spot : at Tamanrasset, in the Hoggar Oasis.

Now, he knew, he had found the right place and the right way of life—for him. So he lived there for several years. He was a good linguist and he devoted his gifts to learning the language of the wild Touareg tribes; many of them came to visit him, and he made friends with them. As time passed he saw he must give up any idea of 'enclosure'. If he was to be the 'Brother' of all he must be at their disposal, whenever they came. He longed to bring these people to the knowledge of Christ, but he saw that for him his work was rather to be that of preparation for the Gospel. So he compiled a French-Touareg Dictionary; lived in prayer, and helped the people who came to him in every way he could, sometimes when simple medical care or nursing, at other times

D

by teaching the women and children little skills which de-
lighted them and made their life pleasanter. He prayed, and
wrote, and waited, being content to be a 'seed, cast into the
ground', and 'buried out of sight'.

It was a very solitary life. A French general who stayed
with him in the winter of 1909 says that no one can imagine
the extreme solitude in which he lived: for months at a
time, he saw no French friends, letters were delayed owing
to postal difficulties. Gentle and courteous, he could be very
firm, for he had 'a will of iron'. For years he lived in this
way, in prayer and humble service. Then, on 1st December,
1916—during a time of political unrest—some strange men
came to Tamanrasset. They seized Charles and bound him;
he waited in silence. In a moment of confusion, seeing some
French soldiers approaching, the man who was guarding
Foucauld shot him through the head, and threw his body
into a ditch.

It looked as though all his hopes and dreams had died
with him. On the very day of his death, he had written to a
friend: 'We can leave "honour" to those who desire it.
What *we* ought always to desire for ourselves is danger and
difficulty.' These were no empty words, for from the beginning to the end of his life, he had sought to know and do
the will of God. Now the 'seed' of his life had literally fallen
into the ground—and was buried. One of his Muslim friends
wrote to Foucauld's sister: 'Charles the Marabout has not
died only for you, he has also died for us all. May God grant
him mercy and may we meet him in Paradise'.

In the heart of the Sahara, in the midst of a fantastic
mountain landscape, on the mountain of Assekrem, stands
the hermitage of Père de Foucauld. It was to this spot that
he used to retire from time to time for complete solitude. He
wrote once to a friend from this place: 'I am completely
alone on the summit of a mountain, which towers almost
above all others . . . the view is wonderful, comprising the
whole Hoggar massif which falls away from north to south,

to the endless expanse of the desert.' He loved this place : its beauty and sense of infinity helped him to realize he was alone with God.

Now Assekrem is a sanctuary, a place of pilgrimage. How has this come about? Why do people—even tourists—want to see the place where the 'hermit of the Sahara' used to live? The answer is this : for many years he had longed for companions in the desert; he had dreams of a new Order, combining contemplation and identification with the poorest, most neglected, and needy people in the world, one in which the Brothers would *live* the Gospel rather than preach it. He often wrote 'home' about this, and his closest friends knew what was in his heart. He prayed and prayed, but no one came. And then, twenty years later, one of the most amazing events in church history took place. A new Order came into being entirely due to his influence, initiating a new form of the 'religious life'.[1]

The Influence of Charles de Foucauld

For several years nothing more was heard of Charles de Foucauld. His death had made no impression; it was just something that happened in the midst of the World War in Europe, in a land so far away that it attracted no notice. Then a well-known writer, René Bazin, wrote a full-scale biography (1921) which aroused a great deal of interest and was widely read. Other books followed. One of them was read by a French priest, Père René Voillaume. He was deeply impressed by the whole story, but particularly by the 'dream' of a new Order, incarnating a new ideal of religious life. He felt this to be the call of God. Others gathered round him, and he became the first prior of the Little Brothers of Jesus.

[1] A recent biography (1962) is *Charles de Foucauld, Adventurer of the Desert* by E. Garnett (Burns and Oates). See also R. Voillaume, *Au Coeur des Masses* (Editions du Cerf, Paris).

In 1933 a small beginning was made at El-Abiodh-Sidi-Cheikh (near Oran) on the fringe of the Sahara Desert. The members of this small fraternity (25 to 30 men) lived there quietly until war broke out in 1939. Then everything slowed down. About the same time two similar women's groups were founded : one in August 1933 (mainly contemplative); the other in 1939, which made a special point of making friends with Muslim women in the midst of daily life. Until 1945 no further expansion was possible.

The turning-point came in 1945, when the Little Sisters founded a 'fraternity' at Tunis, and at Aix the first men's fraternity was founded in the world of industry. From this time forward the whole movement spread rapidly.[1] Amongst the Sisters the growth has been still more rapid. In 1958 there were 200 fraternities, representing some 680 Sisters (of whom 430 were professed). They belong to 46 nationalities, and are scattered throughout more than sixty countries.

This movement is a new and original form of the religious life. Fundamentally it is contemplative, yet it is in very close touch with men and women; its life moves naturally between the desert and the crowd. It is very varied in character and yet quite unique. The only 'Rule' is to 'contemplate Jesus' and to try to follow him in every possible way, especially in prayer, and in loving service to all around, after the pattern of the 'hidden life of Nazareth'.

It is not an easy ideal. Some find the desire for 'contemplation' so strong that they wish they could enter an enclosed order like La Trappe; others are so much moved by the needs of the people around them that they are tempted to put 'action' before prayer. The difficulty, for most of them, is to know how to live in this tension between the two

---

[1] In October 1946 there were 16 Petits Frères, in 1958, 194. At the outset all the Brothers were French. Ten years later 16 nationalities were represented, and 52 fraternities had been established in nineteen countries, in Europe, Africa, Asia and America. Information may be obtained from *Jesus Caritas*, 11 Cité Trévise, Paris 9.

forms of life in such a way that at last it becomes a unity. Great emphasis is laid on the need for silence and solitude. Writing from Tamanrasset Père Voillaume says:

Tamanrasset, and in a very simple way Assekrem, are destined to play an important part in the spiritual life of the fraternities. We cannot regard the fraternities of the Hoggar as on quite the same level as the others. They will have a distinctive and unique part to play, not only for us (the members of this Order), but for the universal mission of Frère Charles. We might say that Assekrem is called to become for the disciples of Père de Foucauld what Mount Alvernia was for St Francis. . . . This is not only because it was here that Frère Charles spent the most fruitful years of his life, and consummated his sacrifice with his own blood, but because the grandeur of the region and the nature of the climate make the Hoggar the desert place most closely adapted to the spiritual message of which it is itself an impressive sign.[1]

Thus it seems that the influence of Père de Foucauld on our own day is as great as that of the great founders in other ages, such as St Benedict or St Ignatius. His message has a peculiar relevance to the needs of our own day. In a world where so many people know nothing of the Christian faith, but are instinctively hostile to it, 'direct evangelization' in the way of preaching and argument is not only impossible, but rather alienates than attracts. This applies to many parts of so-called Christendom, as well as to Islamic and other lands. Precursors are needed, who will gently and quietly prepare the way of the Lord. This work may be described as a 'pre-mission'.[2]

[1] *Lettres aux Fraternités*, vol. ii, pp. 206-7.
[2] A striking example of the direct influence of Charles de Foucauld is the life of Père Périguère (1883-1959). For thirty years he lived alone, among the Berbers of Morocco, regarded as a 'holy man' by them. They flocked to him day after day—he cared for the sick, clothed the naked, fed the hungry, and spent his nights in study and prayer.

The swift growth and expansion of the congregations of the *Petits Frères* and the *Petites Soeurs de Jésus* is the immediate outcome of the life and prayer of Brother Charles. Already these 'fraternities' (which include both priests and laymen) are scattered all over the world: in the Sahara, in Central Africa, in Ceylon, Iraq, Chile, as well as in France and other countries in Europe. All the Brothers earn their living by manual work, sometimes in great insecurity. The majority of the Sisters do the same; occasionally one or two may work in a hospital or an office.

Charles de Foucauld's influence radiates outward through various other movements which are affiliated to the actual congregation itself. As a stone thrown into water causes a ripple of concentric circles, so this spiritual movement continually expands. Round this new Order there is a whole spiritual family, composed largely of lay people. It seems as though the existence of these small 'fraternities', dedicated for life to this mission of prayer and humble service, speaks to people of the present day in a special way.

The influence of Charles de Foucauld can be traced also in offshoots from the traditional Religious Orders. At present, the Dominicans are to the fore in France, and are indeed in the thick of all the new movements. They contribute a great deal on the side of thought and theology through their publications as well as in other ways. The following two instances show this double inspiration: partly traditional and Dominican, and partly due to the main current of renewal that is pulsing through so much of the life of the Catholic Church in Western Europe.

The first instance is the new community of the *Petites Soeurs Dominicaines de Notre Dame*, founded in 1951 by two women drawn to lead a life of prayer together. They settled down very quietly in a small village; soon several others joined them. Today there are about forty Sisters.[1]

This community looks to St Dominic as their original

[1] Bethléem, Vaux-Mery-sur-Oise, Seine et Oise, France.

founder and to Charles de Foucauld for the spirit and order-
ing of their present life. They seek to follow St Dominic,
specially in their fidelity to the contemplative element in the
Dominican ideal and in their emphasis upon theological
study and the 'ministry of the Word' through retreats. St
Dominic aimed at following Jesus in the public life of
preaching and teaching. Charles de Foucauld was drawn to
follow him in the hidden life. This element enters into
much of their practice : in the large amount of time spent in
adoration and in solitude and also in corporate and private
prayer; in the simplicity and poverty of their daily life, earning their living by the work of their hands; in their accessi-
bility to all around them, as they try to be 'missionaries'
through prayer and friendship. They sum up the purpose
of their community under three headings : (*a*) to live in the
desert, hearing the Word of God in silence and solitude;
(*b*) living with their Sisters as in a family nourished by the
Word of God; (*c*) in the world, open to all, sharing the
Word of God with their brothers and sisters.

A similar community founded in the nineteenth century,
which is a vital influence today, is the remarkable 'Bethany'
Congregation. Its founder was Père Lataste, a French
Dominican, who in 1864 used to give religious addresses to
women prisoners in the Cadillac gaol. When he came to
know some of them personally he found that many were
already longing to lead a new life, even while they were
serving their prison sentence. So he kept in touch with them,
and tried to help them when they came out of prison. Then
he discovered that no one would have anything to do with
women who had served a prison sentence; they could not be
received back into ordinary society. So he conceived the idea
of forming a new Dominican Congregation, composed of
nuns, who were to be mainly contemplative, but who would
combine with this the 'apostolic' work of receiving women
straight from prison as their guests, in the hope that they
might be able to rehabilitate them. They were also to receive

women who wanted to live a Christian life after an immoral life in the world. Of course, not all the women who stay there have a religious vocation—any more than among any other group of women. The older women who are 'little sisters' belong to the Third Order of St Dominic.

This congregation has spread from France and Belgium to other countries, including Germany, South America and Switzerland. Father Lataste used to say to women who were haunted by their past life : 'God does not ask what we once were; he only looks at what we are now. . . . God is our Friend, and to a friend all our *mea culpa* confessions are not worth so much as one heartfelt "I love you".'

Another very interesting congregation is that of the *Petites Soeurs de l'Assomption*, founded in 1865 by a monk, Père Pernet.[1] In one sense it is not 'new', but its spirit is very close to that of the new type introduced by Père de Foucauld : it unites the idea of *présence à Dieu* and *présence au Monde*, in a very deep way. In the words of its founder, this community unites two elements : the contemplative and evangelistic. Every Sister should have 'the soul of a Carmelite' and 'the heart of a missionary'—belonging wholly to God, and at the service of the Church for a particular service in the world.

The active aim is very concrete : they aim to serve working people, especially those in need, sickness and trouble, in every way they can. For this they receive a special practical training as nursing sisters, social workers and home helps. People who know these Sisters and have seen them at work say they are very 'human', gay and full of vitality, preserving a certain youthfulness of spirit right up into old age. The secret lies in their life of prayer : four hours a day is spent in worship and private prayer. From a small beginning in 1865 they now number 2,500 nuns, belonging to 27 nationalities, working in France and other European coun-

[1] 57 rue Violet, Paris 15.

tries, and also in the Americas, New Zealand and the Middle East.

The very fact of this current of new life is having its effect on the traditional Orders themselves, who find that they have adapted their way of life to the new trend. One of the most interesting examples of adaptation is that of the *Ancelles* (Handmaids), which is the active (new) branch of a traditional Order, Our Lady of Sion. This congregation was founded by two brothers, converted Jews. Its mission is first of all continual prayer for Israel, coupled with the admission of many Jewish pupils to their schools. A few years before the Second World War the Society of the *Ancelles* was founded as an integral part of this congregation : its expression is, however, very different. The *Ancelles* go through the same training, but when they enter upon their main work they live in small groups, in districts inhabited by Jews; they keep open house, wear ordinary dress, talk at meals and over the washing-up. But behind all their full life is a deep life of prayer, coupled with various kinds of active work as district nurses, social workers, or teachers, by which they earn their living. Every *Ancelle* has an hour a day for private prayer, and a day of silence once a week, in addition to the monthly day of recollection spent together, and the annual retreat. Part of their summer holiday is also spent in solitude and retreat.

Finally, here is another example of the influence of Père de Foucauld which comes from India. A French priest, Jules Monchanin, born in 1895, was regarded in his youth as one of the most brilliant French priests in the country. He worked zealously as a parish priest before he became a professor. He was extremely interested in speculative philosophy and in the religions of Asia. Through Louis Massignon (a friend of Charles de Foucauld) he learned a great deal about Islam, but his strongest attraction was to India. Finally, after many years in France, he offered to go to India as a missionary. At first he worked for some time as a parish priest, but all the time he was studying the thought and life of Indian saints and ascetics. After many years of study and prayer, he came to the conclusion that the Christian message needed to be given to India in the form to which they were accustomed by their own holy men.

Having received permission to found a small *ashram* for prayer and silence, at last in 1950, on the day of St Benedict, he settled down with one companion at the little hermitage of Saccidananda, consecrated to the worship of the Trinity, situated in a grove of mango trees to which he gave the name of the Wood of Peace. So there he lived, dressed in the saffron robe of a Sannyasi, with the Benedictine cross upon his breast. Here he began to exert a spiritual influence which has been compared to that of the 'hermit of the Sahara'. He had fully grasped the mission of Père de Foucauld, and, in addition to the Carmelites, his closest spiritual contact was with the Fraternity of the Little Sisters of Jesus at Trivandrum. He died in 1957. After his death, many people, both Indian and others, testified to the great value of his life and spirit.

Dom Bede Griffiths, O.S.B., wrote thus about him: 'His apostolate in India was distinguished by this deliberate acceptance of a hidden life. It was a way of the Cross, of apparent defeat, and often of incomprehension, but it was also the way which went furthest into the heart of India, and of which we may one day hope to see a rich harvest. Père Monchanin did not expect to see this day, but his work did not end with his death. Perhaps only now is it really beginning.'

5

New Patterns of Christian Living

FROM the days of the Early Fathers down to the present day, 'the Church is always young' is a constant refrain, throughout the long history of decline and renewal. But it is only when we take long views that this seems true. It is true of our own time. In spite of the wars and revolutions of modern times, it is a remarkable fact that both in the Protestant Churches and in the Roman Catholic Church there are signs of striking advance. In many parts of the world, especially in the latter part of the twentieth century, new life seems to be welling up from unseen springs.

A 'Secret Discipline' in Protestant Europe

In many Protestant countries in Europe new patterns of Christian living are emerging. They take very varied forms: some are on a large scale, some are small and intimate, and many are still in embryo. Here are some instances from Germany.

The Kirchentag Movement, inspired by a layman and designed for the laity, came into being soon after the war. Its aim had been hammered out by Reinold von Thadden-Trieglaff, while he was in a prison camp in the Arctic Circle. He conceived the idea of a movement which would lift the Church in Germany out of its former rut and strike out on a new line. 'The Church', he said, 'must not only want to go to heaven; it must also desire the world to be brought under the rule of Christ.'[1]

The first full Kirchentag on this new pattern was held at Essen in 1950; since then, at intervals, it has met in Berlin, Stuttgart, Hamburg, Leipzig, Frankfurt-am-Main and Munich. These gatherings, which are attended by thousands, are impressive; they are always extremely well organized, even to the extent (as at Munich) of enabling 350,000 persons, sitting or standing, on a damp summer afternoon on the Theresienwiese, to be led in silent prayer, in perfect quietness. At them all two elements are always foremost, the claim of Christ over the whole of life, and the centrality of the Bible. No one who has been to such a meeting can fail to be deeply impressed by the quality of the biblical exposition and the eagerness with which it is received.

Another new element in German church life today—although not organized officially by the Church—is the Evangelical Academies. An 'Academy' is not a college, but a conference centre where people of all kinds can meet for a few days and thrash out burning social and religious questions in complete freedom. These Academies were founded in order to reach people who are either on the fringe of the Church, or quite outside it—i.e. mainly intellectual and industrial workers. Conferences are held for special groups of people, doctors, lawyers, journalists, farmers, railway workers and students. Each group is encouraged to discuss the bearing of the Christian faith upon their own particular profession or occupation, and the problems of daily life. It is a basic principle of this kind of conference that the exchange of views should be on the widest possible basis; it is a forum for real discussion between Christians and non-Christians, in which the views of all are respected. The first Academy was opened at Bad Boll in 1945. There are now eighteen Academies in Germany, five of them in the East.

[1] Werner Hühne, *A Man To Be Reckoned With* (SCM Press), is a recent biography of Dr von Thadden.

The movement has spread to other countries, especially to Holland, Sweden, France and Finland.[1]

More closely related to the main theme of this book, however, are the various small groups and fellowships which are springing up spontaneously in Germany; most of them are moved by a desire to find a more 'Christian style of life' and a deeper faith. Out of a number that are known to exist (probably there are many more which are not known) we can give only a few selected illustrations.

There is the *Michaelsbruderschaft*, a men's brotherhood, which began long before the war, in 1931, with 22 members. Nearly all of them were laymen. In spite of all that has happened since 1931 and the set-backs due to the Hitler regime and the war, when the members were able to meet once more they said that a 'kind of second spring-time swept through Germany': the membership is now 700. At the present time two-thirds of the members are pastors or theologians, and the other third are laymen. Essentially this is a quiet intensive movement, aiming at greater reality in public worship and a greater personal discipline in life and in prayer. As its leaders look back over thirty years they can already trace its influence upon various spheres of church life. Its outlook is strongly ecumenical, especially in relation to Roman Catholics.

Another rather different community has been formed at Imhausen. This sprang directly out of the tragedies and sorrows of the war and the Hitler regime. During the war three youth workers had a settlement here for children and young people, but it was soon suppressed by the government. What troubled the youth workers still more was the state of their country, especially the treatment of the Jews and the horrors of the concentration camps. In their great distress they turned with new energy to intercession. Henceforth, this became an integral part of their day's work. Gradually, through the growing number of visitors to week-

[1] See F. H. Littell, *The German Phoenix* (Doubleday, New York).

end conferences in the village, Imhausen began to be known as a place of prayer. Several of the persons at this settlement were in close contact with the resistance movement in Germany, and were thus involved in its tragedies. So it was out of sorrow and sacrifice that the Imhausen community came into existence.

The influence of St Francis has been felt by several small groups in Protestant Germany. They have nothing so large and ordered as the flourishing Society of St Francis in England, but the Franciscan ideal is cherished by many quiet people in smaller groups and fellowships. One of the best known is that founded by Professor Heiler of Marburg: the *Evangelische Franziskanerbruderschaft der Nachfolger Christi* (with the sub-title *Franziskaner-tertiaren*). Most of the members of this fellowship belong to the Lutheran Church. They are deeply impressed by the spirit of St Francis, and they try to live it out as 'tertiaries' in their ordinary life. For, in the words of their founder: 'the Franciscan idea of life is simply that of the Early Church, i.e. the simple following of Jesus, which the world does not understand, to which indeed it is rather a stumbling block than an ideal.' The members have a Rule of prayer, and are very ecumenical in their outlook. They pray a great deal for peace and for the unity of the Church. They try to make friends with people in other communions, especially with the Roman Catholic Church. This group is not very large; its members are scattered throughout Germany, both in the East and the West.

These are only three selected examples, but it seems probable that there are a great many more of these quiet praying groups. The importance of such groups, however small, informal and unofficial they may be, cannot be overestimated. Again and again in history we know that such a group is the hidden spring from which new life flows into a whole community. But as a rule the people who belong to these groups have no idea of this, and would be surprised to learn that their hidden life had any influence upon other people, still less upon history.

Bonhoeffer, whom the Nazis martyred, used to insist on the need for Christians to discover what he called an *Arkandisziplin*, an 'arcane' or 'secret' discipline, which would preserve the mysteries of the Christian faith from profanation. 'Christians living in the world need the nourishment of the secret discipline, and the secret discipline always sends a man back into the world.' He deplored 'the almost complete absence of any genuine ecclesiastical discipline, and the inability of most Protestants even to understand the significance of such disciplinary practices as spiritual exercises, asceticism, meditation and contemplation'.[1]

Catholic Action and Secular Institutes

Externally the most striking movement within the Roman Catholic world in modern times has been the development of *Catholic Action* between the wars. It has also had a great influence upon the inner life of the Church through its emphasis on the need for retreats and the growth of prayer. It has, however, reacted strongly against the tendency to think that 'Christian spirituality' can only be developed in the categories worked out by the Religious Orders. Its main theme, which has become increasingly clear as time goes on, is this. 'It is possible to become holy in and by means of the state of life to which one has been called, whatever it may be—whether as an active Christian layman, as a workman, or as a member of a Christian family. It must not be imagined that this is a "second-class" kind of Christian holiness. Holiness is one, but it must be apprehended by each in the manner appropriate to his way of life, and not in terms that have been worked out within the monastery.'[2] In this connexion it is significant to note the deep influence in these

[1] J. D. Godsey, *The Theology of Dietrich Bonhoeffer* (SCM Press), p. 254. See Bonhoeffer's *Life Together* (SCM Press) for the fruits of his experience leading a community of men preparing themselves for the ministry of the Confessing Church.

[2] *Twentieth Century Christianity*, ed. S. Neill (Collins), p. 48.

latter days of two saints, Thérèse de Lisieux and Charles de
Foucauld, both of whom drew their spirituality from the
Bible itself.

In the words of Prof. Aubert: 'This new and varied participation of the laity in the life of the Church is certainly
one of the outstanding facts in the history of the Church of
Rome over the last forty years.' There is a real and unremit-
ting movement 'towards the Constitution of a genuinely
adult Catholic Laity'. The same writer points out that the
religious life of the laity is becoming increasingly inward.
'A large number of lay people have been returning to the
discovery of the spiritual roots of their activity in the world.
It seems that the process known as the "spiritual quickening
of the laity" is beginning to take foremost place, and this is
much more important than spectacular achievements in the
outside world.'[1]

Behind this main movement of Catholic Action, and the
development of the 'lay apostolate', another still deeper development has been taking place: the growth of *Secular
Institutes*. Although groups of this kind had been formed
during the nineteenth century, it was not until 1947 that
they received papal approval. So in one sense this movement is a new phenomenon in the Catholic Church. From
the outset the Pope insisted that its aim was to be 'apostolic', and that its members would have to learn to 'proclaim the Gospel to the world of the present day in the
language of the twentieth century'. It is certainly contemporary; indeed it has been described as 'the modern institution *par excellence* of the Roman Catholic Church'.

What is a 'Secular Institute'? The name is a technical
term, describing a group of Christian people, closely united
in their common aim, who live a fully dedicated life 'in the
world' (i.e. not in a convent or monastery). It is essentially
a lay movement, although, paradoxically, priests may belong
to it. Some of these 'institutes' are for men, others for

Ibid., pp. 65-66.

women, and others again are mixed. Some are resident communities and others are not. There are two grades of membership: what we should call 'members' and 'associates'. Most members carry on their usual work in the world, and live either at home or in a school or college or in rooms of their own. This means that many of them are very solitary, inwardly if not outwardly.

Every institute has its own central house, with its superior or director or chaplain, so that these scattered members are supported in every way by the mother house. To it they go continually for advice, rest and refreshment, and above all for prayer and retreat. It is the contact with the centre that enables them to live out their vocation in the world. They are admitted to an institute after a long period of preparation and probation. On admission they take the monastic vows, but outwardly they live like everyone else. Yet they never forget that their vocation is as binding as that of any monk or nun.

Some of these groups have actually been in existence for a long time, so it is only natural that they should fluctuate in character. The ones which last are those with the severest discipline; those which are more relaxed tend to fade out. This is not surprising, for the life to which the members are called demands the utmost generosity; that is why the tests for admission are severe, and why the period of training is prolonged.

Already this movement has taken root in a great many countries: in Germany, England, Austria, Canada, Colombia, Mexico, Switzerland, Uruguay, and especially in Spain, France and England. The institutes' life and service are very varied in character: for instance, there is one which includes men, women and priests; its aim is to bring the Gospel into every part of modern life. Its members take a three years' course in theology and kindred subjects; they live in community.

In all these groups the life of prayer is foremost. There is one in France, loosely attached to the Carmelite Order, which consists of persons with a contemplative vocation, but whose life is in the world. Their training is long and testing : two years in a Carmelite convent—as 'associates'—then 45 days each year at the Central House, and after twelve years they come back for a whole year. Meanwhile they undertake such work as seems compatible with their vocation.

Others have a special vocation to care for people in great need, such as women who have served long prison sentences (here they are received into the life of the resident institute). Another institute serves disabled people, and itself consists of the disabled—a service of mutual help on every level. In Paris there is a wonderful house called *Le Nid*, where a team of trained women (members of the institute) receive prostitutes and girls in trouble; their life is that of a family, not a penitentiary. The fruitfulness of this mission of mercy is so great that a cardinal who knows it from within says that it reminds him of some of the most moving scenes in the Gospels. Others, especially composed of doctors, nurses and social workers, care for sick people in various ways, and have a special care for the dying.[1]

The first Secular Institute to be recognized in England (in 1955) is a women's group called the Grail Society. Its central house is at Pinner, on the outskirts of London. This is now a suburban district, but the original farmhouse, now the training centre, is 400 years old. It stands back in a large garden, where quietness can always be found. This institute lives as a family wherever this is possible. But even when scattered, the members work as a team. This is a very cheerful, lively society. It tries to spread the Gospel of Christ in every possible way : through summer schools, study weeks,

[1] Some Religious Orders have also opened their doors to the sick and disabled, or have created special communities for them, in which they too can live out their religious vocation, e.g. *Les Soeurs de Jésus Crucifié*, founded in 1930.

family weeks, through singing and writing, as well as through personal contacts of all kinds. One of its friends calls it 'one of the most exciting things to have happened to the Church in England in this century'. The chapel is the heart of the Waxwell Farm House; it is very simple, light and bare, and is decorated in blue and white and gold.[1]

The girls and women who belong to this apostolic community have an infectious gaiety. 'They know where they are going, they know Whom they serve, they know why they serve Him, and they are infectiously happy in the service they have chosen. One of them describes this society thus: 'The Grail Society, like other Secular Institutes, is always giving not taking. It is cheerful, not glum. It has no truck with fear, it enjoys attempting what the world might describe as impossible.'

At its heart is the life of prayer: some of its members serve mainly by prayer, but most of them are engaged in an active mission. But all know how to withdraw from the noise of the world into solitude. Scattered through the grounds of the centre are small wooden huts, or 'hermitages', with these words on the wall: *O beata solitudo, O sola beatitudo*.[2] This is the Grail Prayer:

> Lord Jesus:
> I give you my hands, to do your work.
> I give you my feet, to go your way.
> I give you my eyes, to see as you do.
> I give you my tongue, to speak your words.
> I give you my mind, that you may think in me.
> I give you my spirit, that you may pray in me.
> Above all, I give you my heart,
> that you may love in me your Father and all mankind.
> I give you my whole self, that you may grow in me.

[1] The Grail, Waxwell Farm House, 125 Waxwell Lane, Pinner, Middlesex.
[2] O blessed solitude! O sole blessing!

So that it is you, Lord Jesu,
Who lives and works and prays in me.[1]

Movements towards Unity

Thus there are parallel movements of a 'secret discipline'
among Protestants and of an apostolate in the secular world
among Roman Catholics; and this unity of spirit is not a
mere coincidence. A clear sign of new life today is the growing movement towards Christian unity. The changing climate in this sphere is so marked that we may well ask :
'What has caused this change?' Doubtless it is due to count-
less hidden currents of prayer—like the Springs of Clitumnus—flowing through people in every part of the Christian
Church all over the world. One main element in this movement is, however, quite evident: the apostolate of prayer
for unity initiated by the Abbé Couturier of Lyons. Not
only is the Week of Prayer for Unity (in January) observed
in more countries every year, but throughout the year this
prayer is going on in monasteries and convents; in the new
Protestant communities; in Anglican cathedrals; in the *Una
Sancta Bewegung* in Germany; in centres like the Ecumenical Institute at Bossey in Switzerland, the new Maison Couturier in Paris, the Scottish Churches' House at Dunblane;
in groups of friends, in homes and in hospitals; in many local
churches; in many solitary places. As these people pray, they
know that 'the walls of separation do not reach to heaven'.
They feel the pain and sin of disunity, and they taste the joy
of that 'given' unity which is a foretaste of heaven.

External difficulties seem as great as ever, yet the existence
of what Couturier called the 'invisible monastery' at the
heart of all communions and the growing personal contacts,

[1] The Secular Institutes are described briefly in *This is Our Life*
(Paraclete Press, 6 Woodlands Road, Bickley, Bromley, Kent, price
2s.). See also Gabriel Reidy, *Secular Institutes* (Burns and Oates), and
J. M. Perrin, *Consecration à Dieu et Présence au Monde* (Desclée et
Brouwer, Bruges).

as well as the influence of the World Council of Churches and the spirit of charity and reconciliation of the Second Vatican Council, are all signs of a new spirit. The source of this new life cannot be better indicated than in Couturier's own words : 'Prayer is a cosmic force. It changes . . . it helps to bring Cosmos out of Chaos. God thus desires to act through us, to create with us, in us. He calls us to work with him . . . Christ being in us, working in us through the Holy Spirit, we are called to labour for the gathering up of all things in the fulness of Christ.'[1]

New Movements

Some further illustrations, which could be paralleled in many countries, must conclude this chapter.

The first is in Italy, at Assisi. In that little hill-town, in the lovely vale of Spoleto where St Francis started a movement which spread into the whole world, another lay movement has come into being. It is called *Pro Civitate Christiana* (PCC). Its founder is a priest named Don Giovanni Rossi. From 1909 to 1921 he was secretary to Cardinal Ferrari, and accompanied him on his visitations in Lombardy. As he travelled about he became painfully aware of the vast amount of religious ignorance and indifference in his own country. At that time it was not possible for priests to speak in public outside their own church buildings. So he thought : 'then the laity must do it'. So he went to the Bishop of Assisi and laid before him his desire to found a 'lay association' for the work of evangelism. He received permission, and at Christmas 1939, with nine companions, the new association was founded.

The very title *Pro Civitate Christiana* suggests the aim of this movement : to bring the Christian message to every part of human life, and to 'give society a soul'. Above all

[1] M. Villain, *L'Abbé Paul Couturier*, p. 300. An English life of Couturier is in preparation for the SCM Press by Father Geoffrey Curtis.

the members want to bring the message of the Gospel to those sections of society which are furthest away from Christian influence, e.g. industrial workers and intellectuals.

Membership of this society is open to priests and laymen. The vocation to this life involves celibacy and the renunciation of other professional work, but these young men and women do not take the threefold monastic vow. They must already possess a university degree, and they must pass the final examination in theology and related subjects established by the Society itself. This association is a purely Italian movement: it is their own people they want to bring back to God. So there is only one centre: at Assisi. The members are called 'volunteers'. Their 'profession' or 'dedication' always takes place during the Christmas season, then they promise to serve this society for life, according to its Rule: 'in order to know our Lord Jesus, to love Him, to follow Him, and to proclaim Him with all their heart and soul and strength'.

They practise poverty by handing over whatever money they have to the association. All receive a certain allowance, enough to live simply, but when they have to go into society circles, they wear good clothes. (There is no habit.) For the laity the age of entrance is between 18 and 30; for priests, not over 35. The centre is called *La Citadella*; its aim is to show that Catholicism stands for truth, beauty, grace, poetry, hope.[1] As the association grows and expands, more and more buildings are being erected. The latest is the 'Christian Faculty', in which young people study for higher degrees in order that they may be able to occupy important positions in public life. The keyword in all this activity is 'Christological', for this means that Christ is really the centre of all piety, and all thought—'a necessary observation' in contrast to the superficial piety of so many Italians. So the Citadel has already attracted, as they put it, the Catholic *élite* in Italy.

[1] La Citadella, Assisi, Italy. A photograph faces p. 65.

The mission of this association is carried out in many ways: through their publications (which include a fortnightly paper, *La Rocca*, and a new translation of the New Testament from the Greek text), and through popular missions in which the lay speakers are both men and women. Behind this activity, as they say, 'Assisi is, and remains, above all a place of prayer'.

Another remarkable lay movement—the *Focolarini*—began in Italy, in 1943. At a recent rally in the Dolomites there were 12,000 people present representing twenty nations and speaking nine languages. This movement developed out of a small group of young women, under their leader, Chiara Lubich. In the midst of air-raids they sat among the damp rocks in a shelter and 'read the words of Scripture aloud by candlelight'. 'These words', they said, 'shone in our souls as never before . . . never had they seemed so *new*.' These girls did not only *read*; they tried to live out what they read. Gradually others were drawn to join them in this enterprise, and soon other small groups took fire and before they knew what was happening a 'revival' had begun: a revival based on 'the Word of Life', in the heart of the Catholic Church in Italy. This revival is still going on and is spreading into other countries, even as far away as Latin America. There is nothing 'separatist' or 'sectarian' about this movement. Its members are loyal Catholics, living 'in the world'. They lay great stress on love in action, in daily life, as well as in social relationships. It is not easy to describe this movement because it is always on the move. It seems to grow by a sort of cheerful and hopeful infection from one small group to another—all of them determined, as far as they can, to do the will of God to the utmost, to *live* the Gospel before they preach it. As their name suggests, this movement is a 'Fire' which is spreading by leaps and bounds.[1]

A community of a very special kind is settled at Charme

[1] Centro Uno, Piazza di To Sanguigna 13/2, Rome.

in the Rhône valley. It is called *L'Arche* or 'The Ark'.[1] It is a lay community, patriarchal rather than ecclesiastical in character. Its leader and founder is Lanza del Vasto, a Sicilian by birth and a Catholic by religion. He is a well-known poet and writer who has been profoundly influenced by Gandhi's views on non-violence. He says it is not easy to define this community, because it 'is like so many things and yet so unlike'. It is not a sect, though some people might think of it as such. It is an *Order*, though again, of a different character from that of the Roman Church. It has a Rule, its members take a vow, and it has its own internal discipline. It combines many opposites: action and contemplation, East and West, withdrawal from the world and identification with it, tradition and devolution. Its religious position is quite original. The founder calls himself a 'traditional Christian', and he is loyal to his Church. Yet as the patron saint of his community he has chosen John the Baptist, 'who was not a Christian'. What he means is that John was the forerunner of Christ, and this community, although definitely Christian at heart, stands at the cross-roads between Christianity and the adherents of other religions. Its purpose is 'to prepare the way of the Lord', in much the same way as was done by Charles de Foucauld and is being done by his followers.

All truly religious people are welcomed to the *Arche*. They can all take part in a life which is based on spiritual discipline, hard work, peace and respect for one another. This means that Jews, Muslims and others are welcome if they are faithful to the worship and spirit of their own religion. Yet in spite of this extreme openness here is a wonderful spirit—deeply Christian, yet full of respect for other forms of true religion. A Roman Catholic priest who knows this community well says that in all the twenty years of his ministry, in various parishes and movements, he has seen 'more men and women brought back to faith and the sacraments at the *Arche*,

[1] *L'Arche*, Bollène, Avignon, Provence.

and more spiritual and apostolic progress made by the companions and friends of the *Arche*, than by any other means'.

Here is the testimony of a Protestant pastor:

The majority of the members of the *Arche* are Catholic, but this is not planned; one of the Companions is a Protestant and takes part in the parish life of our church at Bollène. Some of the Friends who are associates of the community are also Protestants, either from France or elsewhere. The only kind of person who is not received as a Companion or Friend is someone who is fundamentally irreligious. The Rule of the *Arche* covers everyone who practises his or her own form of religion. Two great biblical principles help us to understand the position of this community. There is the covenant of God with Noah, with humanity and with every living thing; this explains its openness to members of all religions, its emphasis on non-violence, and its respect for animals and for nature as a whole. Then there is something of John the Baptist, the prophet who points his own nation towards Christ.

One of the lay movements in England which is nearest to some of the new movements on the Continent is the society known as the *Servants of Christ the King*, founded in 1944. It is a 'cell' movement within the Anglican Church, and consists of a number of small groups or 'companies'. These are united by a common Rule, which each member accepts after the initial period of probation. The aim of the society is expressed very clearly in the Rule:

1. I believe that my life in all its fulness belongs to God, and I therefore reaffirm the promises made for me at Holy Baptism and renewed by me at Confirmation.

2. I believe that God has called me into the membership of a company of the Servants of Christ the King, so that by waiting upon God in prayer, discipline and fellowship, I may do better work for His Kingdom.

3. I therefore hold myself bound by the following obligations and by the Rule of my company:

(*a*) To worship in church and to receive Holy Communion regularly, to keep a definite time for prayer, Bible reading and the study of the Christian faith, and to offer to God my use of possessions, my personal relationships, my time and my actions.
(*b*) To seek through the company to which I belong, and through every means God gives me, to claim all human life for the Rule of Christ, and to draw others into the fellowship of the Church.
(*c*) To be a faithful member of the Anglican Communion, and to be obedient to the unanimous decisions of my company.

A great deal lies behind this Rule; it is more drastic than it looks on the surface. The wording is deliberately restrained, and all jargon has been avoided.

The Servants of Christ the King know that they have been called to live the Christian life as fully as any monk or nun. They know that they have to do the difficult thing of living their lives where they are, in the 'world', with the same high aims as many others who have made great sacrifices. Like the members of Secular Institutes, they put the Kingdom of God first in their lives, within the framework of the Church to which they belong. In their own words, 'they are trying to work from small beginnings to great things, by practising fellowship with a small group of people who are equally committed to this calling; they hope to spread it to the wider circle of the community in which they worship, and then to all whom they meet in their daily lives. They set up a small company with others who are seeking to practise this aspect of the Christian life.'[1]

The theological principles which lie behind their life are three : (*a*) the call to make real in the Church the spirit of brotherly love as in I Corinthians 13; (*b*) the guidance of the Holy Spirit to show them the will of God as they 'offer to God tiny communities bound together into common fellowship, and ask Him to make them usable, and to use them as

[1] Olive Parker, *The New Commandment* (Darton, Longman and Todd), p. 16.

He wishes';[1] (c) they are not called together simply for their own good. Each company seeks to find what it calls a 'common concern', that is, some special service to others which will carry the love of Christ to them. There is no end to the forms of service which are carried out through these small groups. Some members care for old and neglected people; others visit a mental hospital regularly, others at great expense of time and effort help to reclaim 'a problem family'. Others may all be deeply engaged professionally in some work which takes all their time; to them the company is a great support, and their work is prayer.

The members of SCK are aware that the primary witness is that of their own lives, in spirit and in action. That is what will count in the end; and the witness of words comes after that of the effort to lead a truly Christian life. Here we are reminded of the spirit of Charles de Foucauld, and his desire to '*live* the Gospel before we preach it'. A great many of the companies find that their outward 'concern' is often to some service within their own community. Though experience they have come to believe that this is their present vocation : to pray and to work for the renewal of the Church from within.

The feature of the life of the company which is most distinctive and exacting is the practice of 'waiting upon God'. This is essentially a period of silence, followed by discussion, through which gradually the will of God becomes clear, though sometimes only after a long discipline of waiting, sometimes for months or years. Such waiting constitutes the strength of this movement. It means that—as has been proved over and over again—'a company can grow from being a well-meaning group of assorted people to being an efficient instrument through which God's work can be done in the world today'.[2]

[1] *Ibid.*, p. 21.
[2] *Ibid.*, p. 174. The secretary of SCK is Mrs Olive Parker, 225 Archway Road, London, N.6.

Finally, we must note the emergence of some significant experiments within other Churches in Britain and the USA.

The Community Ministry of ministers and lay workers in the East Harlem Protestant Parish in New York has inspired a number of similar experiments in Community Group Ministry in the United States. The Presbyterian-inspired retreat house at Kirkridge in the Appalachians, led by Professor John Oliver Nelson, has become the centre for a largely lay community of those who keep a simple rule, and resort there yearly for retreat. In London, there is now a Methodist Community Ministry at Notting Hill, the members of which belong to a wider association, the Renewal Group. This group, which was formed in 1961, now has 90 members, mainly ministers, pledged to a seven-fold commitment, which includes common discipline and prayer. The group is at present experimenting with methods of implementing a further and more personal three-fold rule relating to devotion, time and money. It is especially concerned with working this out in relation to ministers and their wives together. So far, the group has not any settled community base.[1]

Many English Free Churchmen are involved in the work to establish 'An Ecumenical House of Prayer'.[2] The aim of this is to provide a permanent house and staff, into whose devotional life groups of persons will be invited for Retreats. A suitable house is in process of being secured.

There is a good deal of searching for forms of community suitable to their own denominational ethos among younger ministers in the Baptist and Congregationalist Churches in Great Britain. Groups have been meeting regularly over the last few years. The Methodist Conference of Great Britain has a committee charged with the task of establishing a 'House for Prayer'.

[1] Details of the Methodist Renewal Group may be obtained from Rev. Robin Sharp, Annandale, North End Road, London, N.W.11.

[2] Secretary: Rev. F. N. James, 29 Southdown Road, Seaford, Sussex.

Epilogue

In an early Christian document, *The Shepherd of Hermas*, the Church is presented as a beautiful young woman, but 'her hair was white'. Even then it was realized that the Church is always old and yet always new. The first Christians called themselves 'a new race', for, as Clement of Alexandria saw, 'they must necessarily be new who have become partakers of the new world'. So this new movement of the Spirit which we have been tracing (in a very inadequate way) is another sign that the Spirit is brooding over the chaotic waters of the present age, bringing order out of disorder and peace out of despair. Many of these communities or groups are small and scattered, and to the eyes of many they may seem insignificant, yet they are 'bearers of the seed of unity'. They are an integral element in the life of the Church universal.

Do they foreshadow a great religious awakening? Or are they destined to form a faithful 'remnant' which will stand firm in a time of terrible testing? We cannot tell. But some points are very clear. In whatever part of the Church these new movements take shape, they are all deeply concerned about the following six points.

1. They are deeply concerned about *the state of their own Church*. They see much that is lacking in it, they are oppressed by its conventionality, its mediocrity, its ultra-conservatism, its unwillingness to change, and its indifference to the needs of the contemporary world. They see that the great need is for *repentance*, beginning with themselves.

2. They are aware that 'the Church exists by *mission* as fire exists by burning', and they are all making real efforts to spread the Christian message, through their lives and by their words.

3. They are profoundly concerned about *Christian unity*. It is a striking fact that wherever this new life appears both in Protestant and Catholic communities and fellowships, men and women find each other in Christ and begin to pray and work as never before for the extension of this spirit of unity.

4. They all put *prayer* in the centre. Without God they can do nothing. They restore in their own lives the right relation between prayer and action; for they know that the Church as a whole is languishing for lack of prayer. Prayer for them is first of all *worship*: turning away from themselves to worship the Father in spirit and in truth; and after that, intercession for all mankind—'this thy family'—for which Christ died.

5. They all know the need for, and the value of, *solitude and silence*. They believe that 'society depends for its existence on the inviolable solitude of its members' and that this is not 'just a recipe for hermits, but that it has a bearing on the whole future of man'.[1] This explains why so many of them speak of their longing for 'the desert'.

6. Above all they stand for *single-mindedness*: that is, for holiness—for the life that is absolutely given to God for him to use as he wills.

They challenge us all to live more truly as members of the ONE, HOLY, CATHOLIC CHURCH: that is, in unity, holiness, mission—and the three are one. For God is speaking to us, here and now.

[1] Thomas Merton, *Thoughts in Solitude* (Burns and Oates), pp. 12, 13.

INDEX